T0208504

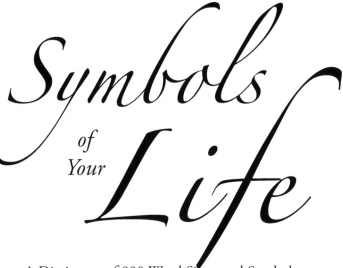

Symbols

of
Your

Life

A Dictionary of 990 Word Signs and Symbols to
Develop Your Spiritual Language with Your Angels and Guides

SARAH PAOLA

SymbolsOfYourLife.com
OpeningYourIntuition.com

BALBOA.PRESS
A DIVISION OF HAY HOUSE

Balboa Press books may be ordered through booksellers or by contacting:

Balboa Press
A Division of Hay House
1663 Liberty Drive
Bloomington, IN 47403
www.balboapress.com
844-682-1282

Because of the dynamic nature of the Internet, any web addresses or links contained in this book may have changed since publication and may no longer be valid. The views expressed in this work are solely those of the author and do not necessarily reflect the views of the publisher, and the publisher hereby disclaims any responsibility for them.

The author of this book does not dispense medical advice or prescribe the use of any technique as a form of treatment for physical, emotional, or medical problems without the advice of a physician, either directly or indirectly. The intent of the author is only to offer information of a general nature to help you in your quest for emotional and spiritual well-being. In the event you use any of the information in this book for yourself, which is your constitutional right, the author and the publisher assume no responsibility for your actions.

Any people depicted in stock imagery provided by Getty Images are models, and such images are being used for illustrative purposes only. Certain stock imagery © Getty Images.

Print information available on the last page.

ISBN: 979-8-7652-4788-4 (sc)
ISBN: 979-8-7652-4790-7 (hc)
ISBN: 979-8-7652-4789-1 (e)

Library of Congress Control Number: 2023923125

Balboa Press rev. date: 12/29/2023

CONTENTS

ACKNOWLEDGMENTS

I would like to thank two women without whom
this book would not have been possible.

My first spiritual teacher and mentor, Mary Jo, started me
down the road to understanding the spiritual language used by
our Guides and Angels. I can't begin to thank Mary Jo for all
that she brought into my life and taught me along this fantastic
journey. She has not only been an amazing soul intuitive but
also a phenomenal teacher for so many through the years. She
will always have my sincere love, respect, and admiration.

My brilliant, caring friend Peggy believed in me and allowed me
to whine like a three-year-old when life was difficult and to cry
on her shoulder through the years. She has been there every step
of the way supporting me. I thank her from the bottom of my
heart for all she has done for me time and again. May she and
her husband have a blessed life through many years to come.

PREFACE

In my years of conducting psychic readings for countless clients and teaching classes and courses on psychic abilities, I found that it helps everyone most to keep the information as straightforward as possible.

Every single person across the earth has intuitive psychic abilities. I'll talk more about that later in the book, but for now, I feel it's important to say that you should never let inner doubt tell you that you don't have psychic abilities. Some already know they have it, and others, as I once did, don't believe they have any such abilities at all but are curious and want to learn more. When I speak of "psychic abilities" throughout this book, I'll be referring to these intuitive psychic abilities that everyone has.

The number one question I'm asked is how it started for me. Have I always been aware of my psychic abilities? That's a firm no! I was raised Southern Baptist—meaning no dancing or drinking, and definitely no psychic abilities. I didn't know of or understand this until I was married with children in my early forties. My journey started with one extraordinary night that I will never forget.

It was the wee hours of the night. I sat up in bed and started talking to an unknown man who was standing in my bedroom doorway wearing blue jeans and a blue T-shirt. I could see him clearly and never once thought it was strange or scary that he was in my home in the middle of the night, standing in my bedroom doorway with my then husband sound asleep beside me. My husband sat up and asked me who I was talking to in the middle of the night. I casually told him I was talking to the man at the door, and everything went crazy. My husband jumped up to run around the house, looking for this man. As he did that, the man disappeared.

That moment completely changed my life and the direction it was going in. Who was the man? I believe he was my Guide. Why was he there? He was there to retrigger my psychic abilities and wake them up again.

After that moment, I began seeing things in daily life, dreams, and waking visions. Considering how I was raised, it was an incredible blessing to have my first, best, and most loved mentor come into my life to teach me about psychic abilities. Mary Jo came into my life very quickly after my middle-of-the-night experience.

I genuinely believe it was the work of my Guides putting Mary Jo's information in front of me to spark my interest in learning more about the psychic world. Once you take your first step on this path, your higher power will bring you the people and tools you need to continue growing and moving forward.

After studying with Mary Jo for a time, I began attending every class I could find to expand my psychic abilities. I have had so many teachers, courses, and training sessions through the years that I've lost count. In each class, the instructors did an excellent job of teaching me to connect with my Guides or loved ones who had crossed over. The instructors would share that it was vital to receive the information but also essential to accurately interpret the signs and symbols the Guides sent. They would give a few symbol examples with interpretations, then sent me home to create a symbol definition list on my own. Creating a symbol definition list was daunting for almost everyone attending these events. People would go home and never develop their symbols list. For many, it became a stumbling block to moving forward and growing in using their psychic abilities.

Many instructors suggested that the students read dream interpretation books. Most dream interpretation books are full of definitions with multiple long paragraphs, each depending on the connotation of the dream. It's challenging and confusing to remember that overload of meanings for one symbol. Thankfully, I had a starter list Mary Jo shared in one of her books.

I began editing her list to fit how I thought about and interpreted each symbolic image and added many more. After several years of trial and error, repeated refinement, and hard work, I finally had a list of over 500 symbols with interpretive definitions. As I did readings professionally over the years, that list grew significantly. That's when I realized I wanted to share my symbols dictionary with everyone, not just students taking my Opening Your Intuition courses or clients. I hope this book will take the hard work out of creating your own symbol dictionary.

In this book, I'll be explaining topics for those who are beginners as well as building on information an advanced psychic will find helpful. I'll also share some of my most thrilling, blessed, and sometimes embarrassing psychic moments as examples rather than loading in extra technical information. I hope to help you avoid a few of the pitfalls I experienced as you move through your spiritual journey.

Symbols of Your Life does all the definition and interpretation work for you. This book is loaded with a dictionary of more than 990 symbols with simple, basic definitions that are easy to remember. I've also included psychic growth information, exercises, examples of how the symbols are used, practical applications, and many personal experiences to help you better understand how symbols apply to your life.

This book is meant to be a standalone guide to understanding and opening your psychic abilities or as a supplement to my online series of courses, Opening Your Intuition (openingyourintuition. com). I hope it helps you take a few more steps forward to opening your psychic abilities and quickly interpreting all you receive from your higher power in your meditations, mind's eye moments, synchronistic events, daily signs, dreams, and more.

I wish you a brighter, happier, and more spirit-filled life!

INTRODUCTION

A Whole New World
Opening Up for You

Many feel they connect with Angels while others feel they work with Guides. There are also those who started out as I did and aren't sure who or what they connect to. I'll share more about that in a later chapter. As we advance through this book, I will be referring to our Guides and Angels collectively as "Guides." Also, as this book is for a planet of amazing people—and there are many cultural, religious, and personal belief systems—I will group all spiritual beliefs, and names tied to them, together as your higher power.

I once read that the language of the brain is symbols. We see scenarios, images, words, and more when we think through situations.

If you're asking what a symbol is, I think the definition on Wikipedia says it best:

> A symbol is a mark, sign, or word that indicates, signifies, or is understood as representing an idea, object, or relationship. Symbols allow people to go beyond what is known or seen by creating linkages between otherwise very different concepts and experiences. Symbols take the form of words, sounds, gestures, ideas, or visual images and are used to convey other ideas and beliefs. For example, a red octagon is a common symbol for "STOP"; on maps,

blue lines typically represent rivers; and a red rose often symbolizes love and compassion.[1]

We are all born with psychic abilities and in our early years we can easily communicate with our Guides and those who have passed on. You will find little ones staring at a fixed point in a room as if they are listening to someone. Other times they reach out and try to speak to someone not there. Odds are they are seeing a loved one you can't see. Those wide-open abilities start slowly closing as we grow in age until they are all but shut down by the time we reach the ages of eight to ten.

When you start opening back up again, it's as if someone turns a light switch back on inside you. Synchronicities are noticed and begin to make sense. You feel your intuition becoming more robust, and you find yourself paying attention to your gut feeling more or having moments of knowing something without knowing how. You've always had these moments, but now you know they're something you need to pay attention to, interpret, and take note of. Having your list of symbol definitions will help you easily work through the interpretations.

Here are two of my favorite true-life symbol examples that I like to share in my intuition courses.

A friend was shopping for a used car and found one she loved. She knew she would have to tighten her financial belt to the extreme, so she sensibly decided to ask for guidance and think it through. On the way home, she stopped to get groceries and accidentally knocked lemons loose, scattering them everywhere. Once she made it home, she turned on the TV, and it seemed every ad had lemons. She emailed me to share her day. Knowing I'm big on symbols, she

---

[1] Wikipedia, s.v. "Symbol," last modified July 10, 2023, 14:59, https://en.wikipedia.org/wiki/Symbol.

asked, "What's the deal with lemons today?" I told her I felt it was the answer to the guidance she asked for. The used car was a lemon. Looking further into the car, she found it had been in a wreck and knew her Guides were correct.

When I was working in the corporate world, on my way to work one day I saw a giant frog on the interstate ramp, another one later on the side of the interstate, and yet another in the ditch by the office parking lot. I knew three occurrences of a symbol in a row meant something essential but couldn't think what it was referring to. At my desk, I looked at my workload and realized there was a project I had been jumping around on. I would work on it then hop off to do something else I thought was more important. I knew this was what the frogs were about. Just as I finished the project, the person who requested it came in ready to complain that it wasn't done. Thankfully, I could tell him I had it right there on my desk for him. It took the steam out of him, and he left with a smile.

These types of things happen to all of us daily, but so many don't understand that symbols like repetitious lemons or frogs are signs sent to us from our Guides to help us navigate our daily lives. Our Guides talk to us through daily moments, synchronicities, dreams, meditations, songs, people, emails, social media, TV, and other events in your life.

Here are some examples. You put a question out to your Guides, then the next day someone on Facebook talks about the same problem and gives a great solution. You are sitting outside and notice a squirrel hoarding acorns in its mouth and realize you may need to hoard your money, or whatever applies, to solve the problem. You wake up hearing a specific song repeatedly in your head only to realize it's answering your question. You go through a day dropping things continuously to realize later it's waking you up to something you are dropping that's important.

I could go on and on with examples, but you get the point. I suggest that you not try to determine how your Guides will answer you. Trust me when I say there are times when they come back with a direct, easy response, and other times when they respond in the most unexpected way that has me laughing out loud and telling the heavens, "I get it."

Now that you are opening up to becoming fluent in the language of symbols, signs, feelings, and touch, you will begin to notice them often. Whether you call it a gut reaction, instinct, or a certain foresight about events that haven't yet occurred, everyone has the blessing of innate intuition that, with some work, becomes stronger, moving you into the psychic realm. All it takes is to put your question out to your Guides and ask for a message to be sent to you.

The responses from the Guides may come to you as a bird flying in circles, a logo on a truck that stands out to you suddenly, a billboard that catches your eye, or a song stuck in your head. The thing is that when you receive your answer from your Guides, you need to take a minute to interpret and understand what their answer is. Keep your ears open because a solution can also come from someone saying just the right thing at the right time when you need to hear it.

Let's say someone is ready to settle down and is looking for the perfect person to share a life with. They meet someone who ticks off all the boxes for an ideal partner. Yet their gut feeling isn't quite right, the signs and symbols they receive are not positive, or they pull an oracle card from an oracle card deck warning them it may not be the right fit. However, they ignore all that and move in with or marry that perceived perfect partner. A couple of years later, they realize life isn't what they thought it would be with this partner and divorce. I would have to say that's taking the more complicated and longer road.

It's crucial to remember that free will is genuine and very real. Guides only send us signs and messages to help us. It's up to us to choose which action we take or which way to go. We all have a path to walk in this life, but we are the ones who determine if it's a smooth path or full of obstacles we put in front of ourselves. Your intuition and symbols show you what's best for you. If you ignore that guidance, you may find yourself taking the longer or harder road to achieve what you want. But it is your road to traverse, so again, you choose.

CHAPTER 1

The Psychic Abilities
You Are Born With

Let's start with the differences among intuition, psychic abilities, and mediumship. I like to think of them as levels. Our intuitive, psychic, and mediumship abilities are each at different levels and depths of connection.

We hear about intuition in terms of a mother's intuition, a woman's intuition, a gut feeling, or a tingle down your neck or spine. And yes, men also have intuitive abilities the same as women. It's simply that many men typically aren't open to sharing feelings, much less their intuitive moments.

All these abilities have been with each of us since birth. We are all born with them. How strong your intuition is later in your adult life depends on how you experienced your childhood and how often you've worked with or used your abilities since that time.

Typically, your abilities are strong from birth until five or six years of age. Many children who have imaginary friends are probably talking to a loved one on the other side or one of their Guides. As we grow and age, we begin connecting more strongly with the physical world and life around us as we continue to lose that incredible connection.

Yes, you read correctly: our Guides are with us from birth. We have a master Guide with us most of our life, and we have different Guides who walk with us through certain times of our life. You may have one Guide who walks with you through love and heartache, another who works with you to develop your abilities, another who helps you through traumatic times in your life, and so forth.

Psychic abilities take that intuition you were born with, open it up more, and help you listen more closely to it while expanding your consciousness and connectivity between yourself and your higher power. In what I call "psychic mode," you typically see past, present, and future moments. The future moments can shift or change due to your free will, changing your mind, or the influence of someone else's actions.

When I talk about expanding the connectivity, I mean taking a deep breath, quieting your mind, and opening yourself to connect with your higher power. You can begin strengthening your connection by going through one or more guided meditations to become more familiar with seeing, feeling, hearing, and more as your connection grows.

Exercise: The Roller Coaster

Here's a quick ten-minute meditative exercise to have a bit of fun stretching your psychic ability. In this exercise, and for all exercises in this book, never anticipate or force yourself to behave or react as you usually do. Roll with whatever you see or whatever happens, and give yourself the freedom to learn something new about yourself as you go through the exercises. It helps many to play low soft meditative music as you do the exercises. Reading through the exercise first, then relaxing and moving through the steps from memory, will benefit you. It's not necessary to stick with the steps I share in the exercises—always go with the flow wherever your Guides take you.

Let's begin.

With your eyes closed, start by breathing in deep, then slowly letting it out. Continue breathing deep for several minutes. The best way to help quiet your busy mind is to focus on feeling and listening to each deep breath as you inhale and exhale. Let go of everything else and focus entirely on your breath.

Imagine yourself sitting in the seat of a roller coaster on the platform about to take off. Notice which row you are sitting in. The coaster slowly begins to move away from the platform and clank, clank, clank upward on the tracks. As you reach the top, you realize you are about to go over the edge of the first drop-down.

What do you do, and how do you feel, as it starts to move over the edge downward?

When you reach the bottom of the drop-down, take a deep breath and open your eyes.

Where you were sitting on the coaster tells you something about how you are currently living: cautiously (middle), afraid to experience life fully (back), or ready for anything (front row).

What you did when you went over the top and dropped down tells you more. Did you raise your hands in the air and yell in excitement? Did you tightly grip the protective bar before you and grit your teeth? Did you close your eyes and miss the whole experience?

The Difference between a Psychic and a Medium

As a psychic, you move into mediumship by elevating your spirit, mind, and energy beyond the psychic to connect with your gatekeeper and reach out to loved ones or others who've passed away and are on the other side. A medium works with loved ones on the other side to relay their information to the client the medium is working with. A medium's gatekeeper protects them from being contacted continuously by their loved ones or other people's loved ones.

Once a medium connects with your loved one, the loved one shares general information about how they lived or ended their life and their personality. I always share with my clients the description given to me by their loved ones of how they were in life, good or bad. Then the loved one will share their regrets and things that pertain to the client's life. Don't be surprised when an angry or difficult person in life begins to express their feelings of care and love.

Clair Senses

Your psychic abilities have a name: clair senses. The word *clair* is French for "clear." Your clair senses are part of your different intuitive, psychic, and mediumship abilities. Typically, the clair senses correspond with your physical senses. While everyone has the capability to use all their abilities, most find they have two or three that are strongest and easiest to tap into quickly. Once your more dominant abilities are working smoothly and are easy to access, you can begin working to open your other abilities more.

I like to call our psychic abilities our internal guidance system. That internal radar will go off on its own to give you a heads-up, or you can tap into it to focus it on the direction you want to receive information. Learning to interpret what you receive is what this book is all about.

The main clair senses are:

> **clairvoyance**, sight
> **clairaudience**, hear
> **clairsentience**, feel
> **clairalience** or **clairscent**, smell

clairtangency, touch
clairgustance, taste
claircognizance, know
clairempathy, emotion

Clairvoyance (clear seeing)

Clairvoyants typically see images in their mind's eye or third eye, similar to the way you would see an image in a daydream. For example, you begin daydreaming about getting a job promotion and mentally picture what that would be like.

As our world is full of visuals (TV, videos, ads, and electronic communication), most of us lean toward being visual and are able to understand an idea best when we see an image.

Clairaudience (clear hearing)

An example of clairaudience is when, out of the blue, you clearly hear a song in your mind that you haven't heard in a long time. My Guides do this to me regularly. The problem for me is that I never remember the words to any song. I may catch a word or two of the chorus, enough to look the lyrics up on the internet, but I have yet to remember an entire song or complete chorus of any song. However, I know that when my Guides put a song in my mind, they are sending me information, answering a question I had, alerting me to something, or sending me loving support.

Not long ago I had a painful moment that hit deep and brought me to tears. A few moments later, I turned on the radio in my car, and the song "Sara Smile" came on. It caused me to be even more teary-eyed because I knew my Guides were right there supporting and helping me wade through the pain.

Clairaudience also includes mentally hearing words, sounds of a familiar voice, noises, or someone speaking a specific phrase to you. The first few times this happens, it may be a bit alarming, so keep in mind: yes, you are sane, and it's your clairaudient ability working through you.

Clairsentience (clear feeling or sensation)

Clairsentience is tied to your "gut" feeling. It's that quintessential intuitive hit you feel from your Guides at different times in your life. It's that heads-up warning from your Guides when something is about to go wrong.

For example, you are walking down a street, and you get that slightly alarming feeling that you need to turn around and go the other way. That's your Guide warning you that danger or a problem is ahead. It's also that moment of thrilling elation when something extraordinary is about to happen.

Clairalience or clairscent (clear smelling)

Clairalience is all about smell. I know my grandfather is with me when I suddenly smell his pipe tobacco at a time when no one around me is smoking a pipe. It's the same when I smell cigarette smoke strongly in my home and know it's my father, since I don't smoke. A clairsentient will smell perfumes, colognes, candles, food, coffee, trash, and more. On many occasions, the smell is associated with a loved one on the other side reaching out to let you know they are with you, giving you an alert or even a wake-up call.

Clairtangency (clear touch)

Clairtangency is also known as psychometry, the ability to receive information by touching an item. However, the information you receive comes to you through one of your other clair senses.

For example, you reach out and touch an antique desk and begin receiving images (clairvoyance) in your mind of the person who owned the desk. The touch (clairtangency) activated your clairvoyance.

Clairtangency/psychometry pulls in any one of your other clair senses to deliver whatever information is available in a well-worn, old, or well-used item you pick up.

Clairgustance (clear tasting)

Clairgustance is something of a rare ability that enables you to taste something you haven't put in your mouth or smelled. It can occur when a loved one, here or on the other side, is reaching out to us or our Guides are sharing information.

Claircognizance (clear knowing)

When you have the claircognizance ability, you have a premonition, a sudden knowing that something is about to happen with no explanation or understanding of how or why you know it. You'll also sense information about others you know and those you don't. Typically, these things pop into your mind for no accountable reason.

When doing psychic readings, I will receive information without seeing the image, hearing the sound, or whatever—it is simply there in my mind to deliver to the client.

Clairempathy (clear emotion)

Clairempathy is characteristic of an empath, someone who can feel the emotions of a person, place, or animal. I would venture to say that most of us have this ability at one level or another.

Empaths leave themselves wide open. They have a strong perception of all emotions around them. This, as well as other clair senses, is why it's a good idea to learn to shield your energy and senses when in a crowded area.

Identifying Your Clair Senses

Now that you have a feel for each of the different clair senses, take time throughout each day to begin working to identify which are your strongest. Keep in mind that you can strengthen your current abilities as you also start adding new ones. It took me some time and work to slowly develop a few additional abilities I didn't quite have the capability for initially.

A great example of how my gut intuition (clairsentience) saved the day comes from years ago when I ran errands to pick up materials for an upcoming business event. While I was out, I took an early break and ran to the local mall. As I got out of my car and started walking to the mall doors, I was hit with a hard feeling in the gut that I needed to stop and not go in. Because my curiosity usually gets the best of me, I moved to the side wall instead of the door and eased around to peek in through the glass doors. Standing eight feet from the doors was one of the owners of the company I worked for. I think my heart skipped a beat as I stepped back and quickly headed for my car.

The fact that my Guide sent such a solid intuitive clairsentient moment told me I avoided a problematic situation and possibly saved my job. This is the moment when we know without a doubt that our Guides are always with us.

Exercise: *The Meditative Cloud*

Here's a meditative exercise you can do in ten to fifteen minutes that will help stretch your psychic intuition and identify a few of your clair abilities.

Find a quiet place to lie down or sit comfortably and relax. With your eyes closed, start breathing deeply, slowly letting out each breath. Continue deep breathing for several minutes. The best way to help quiet your busy mind is to focus on feeling and listening to each breath. Let go of everything else and focus entirely on your breath.

As you breathe deeply, start at the top of your head, and imagine a sheer, soft, white cloud that moves slowly down over your head and face. Relax each muscle as the cloud moves over it. Let the white cloud continue moving slowly down over each area of your body, relaxing every muscle until it reaches the bottom of your feet and wraps around them. Not only does this practice relax your muscles and keep your focus on the exercise, but that soft white cloud acts as your protective psychic shield as you move to the next stage.

Once your cloud is fully wrapped around your body and you are relaxed, bring an image of your personal vehicle to mind. Start by strolling around the outside of it, making a note of all details possible. Then imagine reaching out and touching the door handle to open the door. See if you can feel the handle in your hand as you open the door and move into the front seat at the steering wheel.

As you sit down in the seat, can you feel the support given, the material, and your muscles relaxing as you relax into its support?

Now, reach out and start your car without putting it in drive. Do you hear the engine and feel the light vibration from it? Next, turn on your radio and listen closely to the song that begins to play. Does it have meaning for you?

As the music begins to fade, take a deep breath. Then ask your Guides any question that comes to mind. After a few moments with your Guides, reach out and turn off your vehicle. Step out of the car and imagine yourself again easing back into your current sitting or lying position. Take a few more deep breaths, and open your eyes whenever you feel ready to do so.

As you go through this meditative exercise, and as you go through the next few weeks, remember to refer to the list of clair senses above and identify the ones you currently use. If you use only a few of them now, you will find that as time goes by you have others and can continue to develop them quickly. You are not limited to one or two clair senses. You have and can develop most of them, with a bit of practice and attention to what you do daily.

Many have clair abilities they regularly use without realizing what they are or that they are using them. Opening your mind and spirit to accept and expand your abilities will be a surprising and incredible journey for unforgettable experiences.

CHAPTER 2

Who's Talking to You?

We've already talked about receiving information from our higher power, Guides, and loved ones who have passed on. As I shared earlier, our world is full of many diverse religious beliefs when it comes to defining our higher power and Guides. I urge you to stick with your choice of words for your higher power and trust that's who's talking to you.

Occasionally, a person in one of my intuition courses worries that it may be evil spirits talking to them instead of their higher power. I always explain that if your heart, mind, and soul are in the right place, it will always be your Guides sharing information with you. If your thoughts are negative and you have malice, revenge, or hate in your heart and mind, the odds are it's your ego or pride talking to you. Trust me—your ego can do a number on you.

Our ego and pride are often the number-one problem creators in our lives. They tell us we deserve things no matter what the consequences of obtaining them. They tell us our pride has been damaged, we've been slighted, people are ridiculous or less than, and so much more along this vein. Learning to know when it's your ego voice and when it's your Guides is vital to understanding the signs and symbols sent to help you move through life happier and more smoothly.

Getting control of your ego thoughts isn't always easy. You may want to consider letting them out privately without action on your part. Countless times I've stood in my home and yelled at the mental image of someone who caused problems in my life. It helped get out all the anger, hurt, and frustration, and usually by the time I finish ranting, I find I'm laughing at myself and rethinking how to handle the problem. That's the key to finding yourself at a place where you can eventually think more clearly and listen to your heart as well as any guidance shared by your Guides.

We are often so intent on a specific outcome that it affects the guidance we receive and the answers our psychic tools, such as oracle cards, give us. Strong emotions affect everything around us.

Some feel it's the universe, dimensional entities, futuristic entities, or the Akashic records sharing information with them. If that is part of your spiritual belief system, go with it and name it accordingly.

Nowhere in this book will I suggest that you step away from your core spiritual beliefs and systems. I firmly believe in "to each his own"—as long as it doesn't mentally, emotionally, or physically hurt anyone else.

We all have moments when we doubt, have a minor crisis of faith, and are concerned or curious about whom we are talking to, who is talking to us, and whether it's real or our imagination. In these moments of crisis of faith, we need to remember that it really doesn't matter who or what it is or where it's coming from as long as we recognize that it's helpful and in our best interest.

Initially, my curiosity was off the charts wondering who it was, what their name was, or what they wanted in return for the incredible growth, guidance, and help. I continuously heard from teachers that our Guides would tell us their names if we asked. So many people in the training classes felt lacking that their guide didn't give them their name. If you ask for a name and one comes to you, accept that this is what you are to use for whichever guide you are working with at that time. If you don't receive a name immediately, give your Guide the first name that comes into your mind and ask them to allow it.

In truth, your Guides don't care what you call them as long as it's not derogatory. However, changing it regularly may be confusing for you and your Guide. Give them any name that works for you and stick with it.

It took me ten years to realize that worrying about the wrong things—such as needing to know exactly who was talking to me, what their real name was, or whether I was bothering them—took away from my focus on growing my spiritual abilities and helping others. The worry over bothering them too often kept me from asking for help as I needed it. In truth, no request is too small or ridiculous, and it's OK to reach out to your Guides multiple times a day if needed.

The main thing to remember is that our higher power may share with us that something is not in our best interest, but they will never talk to us using harsh words nor be derogatory. Our Guides love us deeply, are always there for us, and only want the best for us and our life.

Exercise: Meeting a Guide

Here's a meditative exercise to walk you through meeting one of your Guides.

Find a quiet place to lie down or sit comfortably and relax. With your eyes closed, start breathing deeply and slowly, letting it out. Continue deep breathing for several minutes. The best way to help quiet your busy mind is to focus on feeling and listening to each breath. Let go of everything else and focus entirely on your breath.

As you breathe deeply, start at the top of your head, and imagine a sheer soft white cloud that moves slowly down over your head and face, relaxing each muscle it moves over. Let the white cloud slowly continue moving down over each area of your body, relaxing every muscle until it reaches the bottom of your feet and wraps around them.

Now imagine you are stepping onto a path and begin walking forward slowly. Take note of the scenery around you. As you look forward again, notice that your path ahead reaches a crossroads. Once you reach the crossroads, take the path to the right and slowly move forward. You'll see in the distance a beautiful white gazebo with comfortable chairs inside. As you draw closer to the gazebo, you realize there is a person waiting inside for you.

Step into the gazebo and greet the person waiting for you. Most of the time you won't know the person, yet occasionally you recognize a loved one who has passed. Take a few moments to sit in the chairs and speak briefly with this person. Ask for their name. If they don't give it to you, they may be waiting for you to supply one. Feel free to give it a moment of thought then share the name you have for them and ask if you have their approval to use it. Ask one other question you may have for your Guide.

Once the conversation ends, stand and begin moving down your path back to the crossroads. Once there, take the left that leads you back down the path you started on.

As you move down this last section of the path you feel yourself returning to your physical body.

CHAPTER 3

How to Ask Questions

Several key points will help you ask your questions in the best way possible. However, two are most important to remember when you reach out to your Guides intuitively, through oracle cards, in your dreams, in meditation, or when asking for a sign or symbols to be delivered during waking hours with guidance.

First and most important is the state your emotions are in when you are asking for guidance. Our emotions give off intense energy that leaves an energy mark on what we are holding when we are in emotional pain, overly excited, or fired up and angry. Just think of an intensely emotional movie, play, or musical where the emotions portrayed were so intense it brought you, and most in the room, to tears or anger, depending on the emotion. When you are with friends, and one is pouring out their heart emotionally, you also pick up that emotion and feel it to some extent. Even though the emotion had nothing to do with you or your life in either case, it still had an energy to it that affected you.

That same type of emotional energy exchange will affect how you ask your question, how your Guides perceive the question, and how your inquiry is responded to, and will often deliver a muddled outcome. This is why it's essential to wait until you are in as calm an emotional place as possible before you ask your questions.

Second, always ask your Guides a question with the intent that, good or bad, their response is what you need most at that time or whatever is in your best interest. If you start your communication with your Guides by telling them what you want the outcome to be or possibly asking the question so that you are all but leading them to the answer you want, you'll get a very confusing answer to your question.

Here's my embarrassing example. I had been working on improving my psychic abilities for about a year when I decided to positively put out to my Guides that I win the Powerball (you should see my eyes rolling heavenward right now). I pictured the specific numbers, sent out loads of excited energy, and saw myself winning the Powerball and accepting my big check. So I bought a ticket and played those numbers. When the winning numbers were released, I took a deep breath and checked my numbers. The only correct number on my ticket was the actual Powerball number at the end. None of the other numbers were a match. I burst out laughing—technically, I was given my request exactly as I asked for it. I asked to win the Powerball, and I won the Powerball number only. However, I knew my Guides were also saying, "Sorry, it won't work that way."

In other words, I told my Guides what I wanted the outcome to be and gave them step-by-step directions on how to make it happen, then expected them to perform according to my wishes. Our Guides aren't with us to physically manifest every material thing we want. They don't work on command or perform tricks. They are with us to guide us through the stages of our lives and to support us through the good times and above all the rough. They send us symbols and signs daily to help us accomplish the essential things in our lives and to walk a smoother path not full of potholes.

Many people live their lives in a stressed state, unable to find one time that would be better than another to ask their questions. If that's you, you are probably asking, "So how do I get rid of these emotions to ask the question or work with the cards effectively? These emotions are why I'm going to the cards to start with."

I totally understand. I've been in that situation more times than I can count. A few easy ways to shift your emotions are to take a walk outside, watch a comedy TV show or movie, or think of your happy place. Anything that has you laughing or smiling will quickly release the worst of the negative emotions. Then take three or four slow, calming breaths and reach out to your Guides or pick up your oracle cards to ask your question.

You will often receive an answer very different from what you thought it would be. When this happens, take the time to think through the answer carefully to see where and how it fits. On rare occasions, it may take time for something additional to happen within the situation for it to become apparent what the answer is telling you your best action or inaction may be. However, most of the time you will immediately understand the answer you are given.

Other times, you may want a simple yes or no answer. Right there with you! I am the queen of wanting a yes or no to my question. However, I always remind myself that I would prefer an answer that tells me what I need for the best outcome or next step forward.

Let's go back to the relationship scenario. A woman goes out on two dates with the same person and feels like they could be the partner she is looking for. So the woman asks her Guides, "Will I end up in a relationship with this person?" Let's say the response was, in some form, a yes. The relationship develops, but after many heart-wrenching moments, the woman realizes a relationship with this person isn't what she needs in her life. Remember, she only asked if she would end up in a relationship with the person, and that's the answer she received. Nothing in her question asked if she would be happy in that relationship.

So let's look at an alternate way to ask that question. Let's say the woman had asked, "What would be the result of my entering into a relationship with this person?" Odds are an image of a broken heart or something similar would be shown to the woman in her mind's eye, in a card she pulled, or in images during her daily life throughout the next twenty-four to forty-eight hours. While it may not be the simple yes or no she wanted, it tells her something more substantial for her future. It's sharing that if you start a relationship with this person, odds are you will end up miserable with a broken heart later.

If you are having trouble getting your question straight in your head, take a few minutes and write it down, then edit it until you've reached the core of what you really want to know.

Continuously going back and forth on what you want an outcome of a situation to be is also confusing to your Guides. Imagine a child asking for a piece of candy then changing their mind and asking for fruit. Then they go back and forth multiple times. You reach a point where you give up and wait for them to get their thoughts straight and settle on what they want. Your Guides do the same.

Another essential item to remember is to always ask one question at a time and keep the question as simple as possible. Asking two or three questions simultaneously and expecting one symbol or card to answer them all won't work. Sometimes the answer to the first question precludes needing an answer to other questions. If that's not the case, ask each question separately.

Think about how you would ask questions about a new job offer. Here are a few I might ask if I were someone looking for a job.

- Will taking this job bring me forward movement in my career?
- What type of working environment will this job place me in?

- Will I develop positive working relationships in this job?
- Will this job be in my best interest?

It's up to the person asking to determine if any or all of these factors are important, but I would love to have answers to *each* of these questions. You can ask a series of questions for many things in your life and receive much better results than if you ask for a simple yes or no.

The question I often receive is, "If the answer doesn't make sense to me, should I ask the question again?" Occasionally, my poor brain didn't work in the same way as my Guides did, and their answer truly confused me. When this happens, I do two things. First, I look at the question to ensure I was asking it in an easy-to-understand way. Second, I ask the question again, but preface it by telling my Guides I didn't understand their first answer and ask that they give me a different symbol for the same answer that I can understand more easily. Every time I've done this, the second answer from my Guides was easier to understand.

However, if it's simply that you don't like the answer given and want to ask the question a different way to see if you get an answer more to your liking, you will only muddy the waters and your answers going forward may be muddy as well. Again, I have been there and done this too many times to count, and the results were never good.

There will be rare times when you don't know what the symbol you were sent represents or how to interpret it. Check the dictionary in this book to see if the symbol is here, or if this dictionary is not handy, you can always google the word to see what comes up. Several times when my Guides sent me a symbol I didn't understand, I googled to get a feel for what it's used for, or in the case of animals what their life habits or personalities are.

An example of a symbol is the beaver. Beavers build dams across streams to stop water flow. My interpretation of water is emotion. Then you could ask yourself, why am I building damns to block off my emotions? The next question to your Guides could be, how do I take the dam down? Or, what happened in my life that caused me to build the dam in the first place? Believe it or not, many don't know a specific instance that ties to some of their internal blocks.

Exercise: Learning to Do Blind Readings

Here's a fun exercise you can do to stretch your psychic intuition, have a bit of fun, and receive the answer to your question.

Don't forget to check your emotions at the door before you start. You want to be calm and without expectations of the answer.

Have three pieces of paper ready. Carefully consider your question and the top three possible outcomes of that question, including both good and bad. Then write down one outcome on each piece of paper. Fold each piece two or three times so your writing isn't visible. Place them on a flat surface and shuffle them around until you don't know which is which. Move the three papers in a row with a couple of inches between each.

Then hold both hands out, palms up, in front of you. Close your eyes, breathe deep, and picture the white energy flowing all around you in your mind's eye. Now picture pulling that energy into the center of your palms. After a minute or two, many will feel a slight tingly buzz in the center of their palms. It's not a problem if you don't. You'll pull that energy in whether you feel the buzz or not.

Keeping your question in mind, hold your dominant hand over each piece of paper for a few seconds to see what you intuitively feel with each one. You will be looking for either a feeling of warmth in your hand, a tiny electric buzz in your fingers or hand, or a knowing that one is your answer. When you've settled on which one feels right for your question, pick it up and read it to see your answer.

When I did this in some of my in-person classes, people were always surprised at how easy it was and how great it was to know they could use their psychic abilities in this way.

CHAPTER 4

Numbers, Colors, Creatures, and More

Everything in your indoor and outdoor surroundings—including pictures, TV, movies, magazines, social media, numbers, colors, animals, fish, reptiles, birds, and more—can be used to deliver answers to the questions you ask your Guides. Your Guides will also send you warnings or guide you towards something helpful with messages sent to you daily using any of the above.

Painting Our World with Color

Our lives are painted with color all around us. Everywhere we look, whether in nature or among our manmade comforts, we are surrounded by color. Once you grasp the interpretation of colors, color will allow you to fill in many details about people, environments, moods, and more to give you valuable input daily.

Colors on walls generally affect those who occupy the room. Studies show that rooms painted with intense reds, oranges, and yellows often induce feelings of stress causing people to be more tense when in the room for a time. They also show that blues, browns, and greens are more calming, grounding, and relaxing. At the end of the Symbols dictionary in this book, I offer my interpretation of colors, and you can use that as a reference for the following.

Imagine you are walking into a meeting. As you sit down at the conference table, take a moment to look at the colors each person is wearing. If someone at the meeting table is wearing red, odds are they will make passionate bold statements, be more aggressive than others, or possibly try to take command of the meeting. Someone wearing a pale blue shirt will be the peacemaker with calming ideas or input. Someone wearing light yellow will be the person coming up with ideas and suggestions.

That doesn't mean these people are always like this, but they probably chose unconsciously to wear the color for the meeting as a result of their mental state or emotional mood. The same thing applies to what you pull out to wear for the different moments in your life. That's why it's always important to consider why you are leaning towards a particular color to wear and to examine whether it's right for what you want to accomplish that day. Ask yourself, why do I feel the need to wear red? Do I want to stand out, get attention, or be more aggressive? What color do I want to represent me today?

Look down at the color you are wearing right now. Does it say something about where you are mentally and emotionally right now?

It's easy to scan a room and get an idea of the type of people you are dealing with, their moods, and any potential people you may want to steer clear of.

Colors do the same thing for us in all areas of our life, from vehicles to homes to clothing to signs displayed on businesses. For instance, while shopping for wall paint colors, you may be in a bit of a depressed mood, so you reach for the bright yellow paint because it lightens your mood. Later, when you are in a happier mood, suddenly that bright yellow is too glaring and doesn't fit the mood you actually want for the room.

When you continuously feel drawn to a particular color, stop and ask if this color symbolizes something you need more of in your life or if it's a warning of some type. While traveling on vacation, I walked into a store and was drawn to a shelf full of blue home decorating pieces. I found five items I wanted to purchase, but having them shipped home was costly, so I had to pass on the purchase.

However, when I was back home, I found myself continuously looking for blue pieces for my home. Blue represents calm. That's when I realized my Guides were directing me toward a peaceful and calm environment I needed in my life at that time.

Note also that initially I was drawn to five blue items. The number five represents change. My Guides weren't just directing me to what I needed, they were sharing that I needed the change.

With each shade of blue item I purchased, my home became more of a relaxing haven, which helped me to let go of my hectic work life.

Each color has an energy and vibration that affects everyone whether they realize it or not. Color has the capability to shift moods, incite aggression, or ignite your imagination. Knowing and interpreting colors will benefit you through each day of your life.

All Earth's Creatures

Our Guides use our life experiences, how we feel about things, and how we think to determine how best to send us needed messages.

For instance, I dislike snakes intensely. I avoid snakes or images of snakes like the plague. Any time I find myself going through a day or two with images of snakes popping up regularly or a snake coming to me in a dream or meditation, I know my Guides are telling me that somewhere in my life is a snake of a person about to strike out at me. However, if I were someone who adored and kept snakes as pets, my Guides would use that image in a completely different way.

Your Guides will always find a way to put what you need to see or know in front of you.

Every day you step outside, you see some creature—a bird flying overhead, a lizard running past, someone's dog in a yard—or you get buzzed by one insect or another. Our earth's creatures are everywhere. So it's not about seeing them around you daily but about seeing them repetitiously or when they are doing something unusual or different around you.

Earlier this year, a tiny sparrow flew right up to my office window. Until that point, I hadn't noticed it flying around. It banged into the window, and then flew back up and started pecking at it repeatedly. My usual interpretation for birds is that they are messengers. As soon as I acknowledged that I must have missed a critical message or there was one heading my way that I needed to pay attention to, the bird flew off and didn't return.

A year or so back, a squirrel kept loudly running up and down a tree in the backyard, then ran up in the grass right in front of me and raced back to the tree. That's when I realized it was foraging and saving food in its cheek. I interpret a squirrel as storing or hoarding. Since it was storing food needed for the future, I knew my Guides were telling me I needed to hoard my finances for something that was coming. And yes, they were right.

Last spring and summer, lizards kept popping up inside my house. The first one or two were irritating, and then the next three or so were entertaining as I ran around trying to chase them out the door with a broom. For me, lizards represent regeneration, since they can regrow their tails. They also represent change because they can change their colors to blend in with whatever they are on. My Guides were clearly telling me that a regenerative change was heading my way.

25

There are other times our Guides send us messages through animals in a different way. Many years back, I was struggling with many changes I needed to make in my life. As I was walking out the front door in tears, trying to decide my next steps, I stopped in my tracks. A beautiful feather slowly drifted down right in front of me, not five inches from my face, to the ground. Feathers have special meaning for many as feathers from heaven. They are interpreted as divine blessings or guidance from our Guides. At that moment I cried even harder, but with joy, as I knew my Guides had sent that feather to tell me they were with me and everything would be all right. In the next moment, I had to marvel at the Guides' timing to have a bird fly overhead and drop a feather that slowly drifted down right in front of my face. As I said, a blessing from heaven!

These are just a few examples of how our Guides work with us daily to show us things heading our way or problems and situations in our lives we need to address or to let us know they are with us as we navigate life.

Numbers, Numbers, and More Numbers

In the world right now, we have numerology, angel numbers, our own interpreted version of numbers, and our lucky numbers.

Let's start with numerology. Numerology has been around for thousands of years and came into being when the Greek mathematician and philosopher Pythagoras discovered the correlation between numbers and musical notes. Pythagoras felt everything in the universe could be explained by numbers and the vibrations he associated with them. He also believed everything could be added down to be represented by a single digit.

This is a very different type of addition than what we normally use in the math we were taught in school. In our regular math, we added

8 + 8 and got 16 as the final answer. Using numerology, you take that 16 one step further and add the 1 to the 6 to get 7 as the final number. Then you reference the generally accepted numerology interpretation of the 7 for its meaning. The basic interpretation for the numbers 0–9 used in numerology is included in this dictionary.

Angel numbers are entirely different from any other standard or spiritual number system. The angel number concept was created by a spiritualist who later became a born-again Christian and stepped away from this philosophy. Initially, she felt that multiples of the same number were significant to pay attention to and interpret. For example, 11:11 or 1:11 on a clock had a particular meaning. It's challenging to find the original person's number interpretations. Since there was no longer anyone in control of the angel number concept, many people began bringing their own interpretation of the numbers. I found six very different interpretations for the number 222 in one online search. For this reason, I recommend that you not rely on a particular internet interpretation for angel numbers unless you already have a list you utilize.

With so much confusion around what each angel number represents, I only partially stepped into the angel number concept and have not included them in this dictionary. I did relate to multiples of the same number being notable and viewed them as a more powerful version of my basic number interpretations. You may want to do the same, create definitions for them on your own, or exclude them completely.

And finally, your numbers. For most of my life, I viewed the number 7 as lucky. Later, the number 3 became important to me. We all have our unique numbers with our own interpretation of what they represent. At the end of the Symbols dictionary, I offer the numerology list and a list that combines numerological and personal interpretations, along with some of the typical numbers people hold as special. Just as you will do with every word in the dictionary, always adjust the meaning to fit your interpretation of the numbers or take them off your list entirely if you don't relate to them at all.

You should hear me laughing right now as I reflect on my revelations with numbers. I went a bit overboard learning to sum numbers the numerological way. As a heads-up, doing this repetitiously to get comfortable with the unique way to sum numbers in numerology may affect your regular math skills.

Several nights in a row, I woke, checked the clock, and almost immediately drifted back off to sleep. Around the third or fourth night, I realized this always occurred right around 5 a.m. I knew my Guides were giving me a heads-up that change in some area of my life was coming, and I stopped waking up.

I remember another time when I was struggling with a significant decision to let something go in my life, so I put it out to my Guides to help direct me to the choice that would be best for me. Almost immediately the number 9 was coming up everywhere. For me, 9 represents endings. I must admit, closing that chapter of my life was the best choice I have ever made.

You put a question out to your Guides, and later as you are driving down the road, even though you never pay attention to billboards, suddenly you see a number on a billboard that all but jumps out at you. Odds are, that number is your answer.

Exercise: Numbers

Let's have a little fun doing a quick exercise with numbers.

Completely relax in a quiet place. Begin taking those deep breaths, and briefly shield yourself with the white-light cloud as you continue focusing on your breathing.

As you become fully relaxed, ask your Guides to send you an image of one number to show what you need to do most at this time to benefit your life. Once the number comes to you, begin the journey of breathing to return to where you are now.

If you saw the number 1, it's possible they were sharing that a step into a leadership role is what you need most now. If you saw a 2, maybe you need to find more balance in your life between all the things in it. If you saw a 3, perhaps you need a creative outlet, and so forth. If it was a double-digit number (example 24), add it down to one number as your final answer (2 + 4 = 6). Check the dictionary for the interpretation of this number to see how it may apply to your life.

There are so many ways our Guides send valuable numbers into our lives. They appear on billboards, license plates, clocks, phones, and more. It's the same as with animals. When numbers come to you multiple times, in a unique way, or out of the blue, that's your Guides asking you to pay attention.

CHAPTER 5

Grounding, Shielding, Gratitude, and Forgiveness

I can't express enough what a difference keeping yourself grounded and shielded daily will make in your life. That's why shielding is at the start of each meditative exercise in this book. In the first few exercises, I go more in-depth with it to help you become familiar with the process.

Shielding takes only two to four minutes. It starts with deep breathing as you focus on listening to your breath go in and out. As you relax your muscles, bring white light in the form of a cloud (or whatever form you prefer), over the outside of yourself and into the center of yourself through the top of your head. While I chose to use a soft white cloud in most cases, one of my first mentors liked to picture herself as an empty vessel filled with a white substance as if pouring milk into a bottle. So feel free to use whatever means you are comfortable with to fill yourself inside and out with white light.

You can quickly fill yourself with the white light, or take as long as you need to feel secure that you are shielded. You can do it in thirty seconds or take several minutes. It's entirely up to you and your preferences or the time you have to do it in.

Starting every day by shielding your energy lessens how much emotional overload you pick up from others, helps you minimize others crossing your boundaries and better handle your own triggers that others may typically set off, and keeps you from leaking your own energy to others. It will allow you to support others yet not carry the weight of their problems or illnesses, both mental and physical.

Grounding yourself is basically finding balance in as many areas of your life as possible, including physically and mentally. No matter how hectic life is with family, friends, and work, try to find time for yourself, your hobbies, and the things you enjoy doing. As overly hectic as many of our lives are, you may find yourself continuously saying that you don't have the time. Every time you say this, remember that you are no good to those you care for or work for if you don't find balance for yourself.

Even if all you do is kick your shoes off and walk barefoot in the grass or dirt for fifteen minutes as you breathe deep, you will be amazed at what relief it gives you. Remember to avoid ant piles and not think about work, the latest family crisis, or other problems. Think about your environment, say a short peaceful mantra, or bring beautiful images to mind.

It's for you to find what gives you that grounding feeling, peace of mind, and balance. Then work to make sure you take time daily to enjoy it.

Gratitude for all you receive—your Guides' help, each magical moment you are blessed with, and every moment of loving care you receive from others—will help you open up more to your psychic abilities and connect with your Guides more effortlessly. Just the actual deep sensation of gratitude that blooms inside you for a moment is an incredible feeling to experience.

But trust me when I say your Guides will quickly know when your energy doesn't reflect a true feeling of gratitude. Just saying the words or expressing the sentiment doesn't gravitate up to your Guides. The sincerity in your feelings is always what makes the difference and is key when working with the Guides.

At the same time, they understand and forgive our human feelings of despair, depression, anger, and other negative emotions. They will work to help you move past every moment of them all to reach a better place in your spirit, heart, and mind.

Trust that your Guides walk with you daily through every good, bad, happy, or sad moment of your life. Reach out to them whenever you need them and they will be there.

CHAPTER 6

Rules of Engagement

If you are a beginner on the psychic path, as your abilities grow and you feel comfortable with your ability to interpret the signs and symbols sent by your Guides, you may want to start doing practice readings for your family and friends. I encourage you to have fun practicing your abilities and answering questions for those who are open to and agree with it. The main thing for beginners and those working in this field to remember is that it should be a relaxed and comfortable exchange. Keep it as lighthearted and caring as possible.

To this end, let's review a few best practices that apply to anyone who interprets signs and symbols for others.

Best Practices and Ethics

Here are positive practices I would encourage you to do.

- Stress that we all have free will and that all outcomes can be shifted through changes in life or free will.
- Cultivate a positive attitude toward yourself and others. It will genuinely help you open your psychic abilities more deeply.
- Add grounding activities to your daily practices.
- Definitely shield before doing each reading.
- Keep gratitude in your daily thoughts and feelings.

- Forgiveness may be difficult at times, but it is always an amazing release for your spirit when you let present and past pains go.
- Take a moment to connect to the person you are doing a reading for by doing a short deep breathing moment for both of you. It will help relax you and the other person, who may be a bit nervous about the experience.

But there are also some things that I would caution you not to do.

- No matter what you sense, *never predict someone's death.* Period. No excuses, no exceptions. I've been asked the question several times in my career and had to share clearly that I will never answer that question for anyone.
- Don't play doctor. You can share what you sense as a weak area in the body, but always direct someone to talk with whatever type of doctor they typically see.
- Don't exaggerate what you see or sense. You can expand your interpretation a bit with a deeper explanation of the meaning, but never make it more or different from what it is.
- Don't just tell someone what you think they want to hear if you aren't receiving any information from your Guides or psychic tools. Be honest and share that you aren't receiving any information on the question. You can try asking the question in a different way or move on to a different topic.
- Never force what you see or sense on someone whether you know them or not. For example, if you briefly chat with a stranger in a store and don't know them but have a strong psychic moment hit you about them, don't act on the urge to share it. Even if it's family or friends, if they are not open to it, walk away and let it go.

- No matter how little or much you've been working with your psychic abilities, always keep working to open and improve your abilities. It's a beautiful and fulfilling lifelong process.

CHAPTER 7

Using Symbols and the Symbols Dictionary

The more you refer to it, the more you'll find your symbol dictionary is helpful daily to interpret and understand the signs and symbols your Guides send you. You will quickly begin to see how often your Guides reach out to you and walk with you through your days.

First and foremost, take time to make these symbols and definitions your own as you begin to use them in your life. Below every symbol and its definition, you'll see a line below with the words, "My definition", and a blank line to the right. Use the blank line to tweak or completely change the book's definition to better fit your interpretation of that symbol.

Your Guides use what's in your mind. They feel what you feel and how you think about the different manmade items, colors, numbers, living creatures, or things in nature. Your mind is their reference book for how to speak to you with the different signs and symbols in daily life, receiving information for yourself and others, in your meditations, and in your dreams. How you interpret everything is unique to you.

Second, and just as important, not everything is something. When I first started down this path, I was so excited by the whole process and had so much fun working with my Guides and symbols that I took everything that came my way as a sign or symbol representing anything and everything. I reflect on it now and realize how crazy I took off with it, but I quickly realized that only some things in my line of sight were an actual message. As I shared earlier, it needs to come your way multiple times or in a unique way.

A friend of mine called from the car one day to share a problem with me as her husband was driving them down the road. She had just asked what I picked up on her problem when I heard her excitedly tell her husband to look at what was on a billboard they were passing. In that moment, the billboard had given her the perfect answer to her problem. Just one more simple moment of Guides reaching out to help.

If you have particular things that mean something special to you, like finding a penny heads up, go with it. I'm the penny person. Finding a penny has been special to me since I was a little girl. I'm sure you won't be surprised to learn that my Guides occasionally talk to me by putting them in my path.

Many years back, when I was out of town on a business trip, I was sitting on the hotel bed one evening with a new deck of oracle cards, shuffling and getting used to them. In complete honesty, I was in a bit of a depressed mood over the company I worked for at that time. I was asking my Guides questions using the cards and getting nonsensical answers, not realizing my lousy mood affected the outcome. Being new to working with my Guides and the different psychic tools, in sheer frustration I stopped and got angry, telling my Guides that maybe all this psychic stuff was not really something I could do.

The next morning, I boarded my plane to fly home. As I was sitting down in my seat, I realized there were twenty to thirty pennies scattered on the floor under my feet and around my seat. I gasped, started laughing, and burst into tears of instant joy. Of course, the people around me were raising eyebrows at my outburst and probably questioning my sanity, but I knew my Guides were telling me they were there supporting and sending me much love. That was a defining moment in my spiritual journey. A few days later, life started turning around for me, and I will never forget that incredible moment given to me, which literally took my breath away.

Absolutely have fun learning, interpreting, and using your symbols. Just don't become obsessive with it. Trust me when I say it's very easy to do.

If you have friends or family with the same interest, create a small group to share and discuss the special moments that occur as your growth progresses. But try not to let their interpretations influence your own. Once you settle on a definition, stick with it. This is how your Guides will use it going forward for you. That doesn't mean you can't change it in the distant future and share that change with your Guides. It simply means you shouldn't continuously change your definitions. You won't be able to keep track of your interpretations any more than your Guides will.

And a third point. Every definition has two sides to it, the positive and the negative. As I shared earlier with the snake example, it all depends on the question or situation being discussed and your own personal thoughts or feelings on it, and on how the sign or symbol was sent, how it was received, and any feeling or emotion your Guides sent with it. For example, in the Symbols dictionary, I've listed the definition for squirrel as "to hoard." Depending on the question, that could mean you need to hoard your money or that you don't need to hoard something like old or non-essential things. With the squirrel, I see it with a loaded cheek (hoarding) or I see it throwing debris out of its nest (not hoarding). That's both sides of the coin for a squirrel for me. It always depends on how you see the image.

Most of the time I see more than just a stationary image of a symbol in my mind's eye. It may be something different for you. So in compiling the dictionary, I have put both sides of the coin in some of the definitions, but not all. You can easily edit and add your own on the blank line.

Here are ten tips for working with the Symbols dictionary.

1. **Universal symbols**. A few symbols are commonly viewed as universal. Water is an excellent example. Most psychics will tell you that water represents emotions. I struggled with this at first but soon realized that water flows just as our emotions flow. Also, water goes through many states, such as liquid, freezing (solid), and boiling (gas). However, if you really can't wrap your head around that definition or others and continuously gravitate to a different interpretation, then it's best to go with your definition.

2. **Phrases and expressions.** I often think of family sayings or the different phrases and expressions I grew up with. Some of those phrases and expressions may only resonate with me and others from the American South. So it's entirely possible you won't be familiar with a few of the expressions I use in the dictionary, but I encourage you to write in your own phrases or how you interpret that symbol.

3. **Cultural interpretations.** Only rarely do I list interpretations that are historical, tribal, or from cultures around the world. As an example, the culture of Indigenous Americans has very distinct interpretations and meanings for animals and nature, as do many other cultures in the world. If you are immersed in a culture and its interpretations, it may be best for you to use your interpretations.

4. **Body parts.** For arms, legs, hands, and other human body parts, one of the interpretations listed will be simply "body part." Some body parts have symbolic meanings, which I

include in the definition. It's all in how you see the symbols or what type of question you are answering. It may be that this specific body part needs healing. If you are answering a health question, the body part you see will be referring to the health of that body part. I'll typically address a body-part symbol by asking if they have problems with that body part, and then I follow up with what may be needed next for it (such as a doctor). I can't count the times my Guides suddenly made a body part of mine ache to let me know it was a problem for the client.

5. **Musical instruments.** Even though I put more than one musical instrument in the dictionary, typically all musical instruments overall show the person has musical ability. Keeping that in mind, you can share the instrument you saw and share that it may not be their instrument of choice but points to their musical ability. Other times, depending on the question, the instrument itself will have an alternate interpretation.

6. **People and historical figures.** I often see the faces of my family or friends pop up during a reading. When that happens, I know my Guides are referencing that person's personality or a similar moment that happened in their life comparable to the question the client is asking about. I've also had historical people like Genghis Khan, Jesus, Julius Caesar, and Albert Einstein show up. I interpret these images by what that person symbolizes to me. When I'm doing a reading, I share who it is I'm seeing and give my interpretation, then open it up for them to share their thoughts on the person. At the end of the dictionary, I provide space for listing your own symbols, so be sure to include people you know and historical or mythical figures.

7. **Not everything is beautiful.** At the end of each class in my Opening Your Intuition course (openingyourintuition. com), I like to ask the participants to define six words, using

the first thing that comes to mind. One student who was particularly psychic would always go immediately to the interpretation "beautiful," then flounder trying to reach past that to a more distinct interpretation. So much in life is indeed beautiful to look at, but that interpretation covers too many things and narrows down your interpretive capabilities significantly. Always reach for the interpretive meaning more than the appearance of each item.

8. **Words written out.** Not long after I started interpreting symbols and answering questions for others, I began to use multiple clair abilities in the same reading. I would receive mini "video clips" that told a brief story. I would feel low-level pain in my body that corresponded with the client's aches and pains. I would see words written out. The key when given spelled-out words is to avoid blurting out the word right away, as I mistakenly did more than once. Take a moment to see whether the word itself is the answer or you need to interpret it.

9. **Tiddlywinks.** When an item or image is not in your dictionary and you can't figure it out, try this. For Tiddlywinks, you use a one-inch disk for popping smaller disks into a small cup if you're lucky. When the image came up in a reading, I had no idea how to use it and asked my client if they played Tiddlywinks as a child or could relate to it. They were as blank as I was. I left it with my client to see whether it might ring any bells later for her and moved on with the reading. But not knowing what it represented plagued me for weeks. Finally, I reached out to my Guides and asked them not to use it in a client reading again until I figured it out. I still do not have a definition for it, but fortunately, they have not used it since. You can do the same. If a particular word or image is difficult for you to interpret, move past it and work with what you can interpret. You can ask your Guides to bring you an interpretation or not to

use it until you work through its meaning. If you find that nothing ever comes to you for it, let it go and mark it off your symbols dictionary list.

10. **Receiving.** It's helpful to remember that each word can be used in different ways in many areas of your life. When I shared this dictionary with someone recently, they tried to relate the words and definitions to dreams only. While most words in the dictionary can easily relate to things in dreams—there are also words for those who may be using them to receive information from their Guides to answer questions for themselves or others. If you are asking your Guides a question about a particular person and they show you a baseball field, they are probably telling you that person is active in that sport. Seeing a baseball field in a dream is only helpful if you pay attention to what is happening on the baseball field. Another example is my use of the words, "time of year", for several definitions. If you ask your Guides when something is going to happen, you may receive a holiday or season as an approximate time of year. As you are drifting off to sleep and ask your Guides to show you in your dream when something will happen, they may use a time frame in the same way. When making the definitions your own, remember to keep the different possibilities of how it's used open.

11. **E-books**. For those of you who purchased an e-book, feel free to print the dictionary out and add your interpretations that way. If you have Adobe Acrobat Pro, or a program similar to that, you can also send them to print and choose PDF in the printer box to save and edit the pages. There are a few other ways to printout the e-book dictionary, but I'll leave that for you to explore further.

You don't have to review and edit all the symbols in this dictionary all at once. You can do one a day, ten a day, ten a week—whatever time you have to navigate your symbols. It's helpful to picture each symbol in your mind as you work through its definition and every time it comes up for you afterward. This will help your Guides bring it easily and quickly to your mind in the future. There will be times when an item has a meaning for you but does not appear in this dictionary. I left space at the end of the dictionary for you to list additional symbols with your own definitions.

Above all else, take your time and have fun with your dictionary. When I started out, as I moved around my house, work, or traveled, I would glance at an item and think the definition for it. It became a fun game for me.

And remember: always live each day with your eyes and mind open to the world, not focused so tightly on your worries and problems that you don't see who or what's around you. If you live mired down in your problems, you may miss some of the daily signs and symbols your Guides send your way to help with those problems.

YOUR SYMBOLS DICTIONARY

As you begin working through your symbol dictionary, remember that your Guides use how you think and feel right now to determine how to communicate with you. When you move through life, you will have shifts in how you think and feel due to happy, painful, or exciting moments that occur. As you evolve through the years, your interpretations of your symbols may evolve and change with you. If this happens, I recommend you share the change with your Guides and make a note of it in your dictionary.

As a reminder for e-book owners, feel free to print out this dictionary in any way you are able to and add your interpretations or new words.

Under every symbol and its definition, you'll see a line with the words, "My definition", and a blank line to the right. Use the blank line to tweak or completely change the definition to better fit your interpretation of that symbol.

Symbol	Meaning

A

ABDOMEN, the stomach

unable to digest something; stomach problems

My Definition _____

ABORIGINE

primitive; original to; primal

My Definition _____

ABORTION

ending a new life or opportunity

My Definition _____

ABYSS, standing at the edge of

looking deep inside oneself; facing buried fear

My Definition _____

ACE

having an ace up your sleeve; an alternate plan

My Definition _____

ACID

something eating away at you

My Definition _____

ACORN

small beginnings; the kernel of a new idea

My Definition _____

ADVERTISEMENT

a need to advertise or promote oneself

My Definition _____

Symbol	Meaning
AIR CONDITIONER	chill; cool down
My Definition	_____
AIRPLANE	travel by plane; pilot, flight attendant; works at airport
My Definition	_____
ALARM	warning; beware
My Definition	_____
ALCOHOL, bottle of	addiction of any type
My Definition	_____
ALIEN	something unknown to you
My Definition	_____
ALLIGATOR	something that could eat you alive
My Definition	_____
ALTAR, being on an	self-sacrifice
My Definition	_____
ALTAR, kneeling before	something humbling, that brings you to your knees
My Definition	_____

Symbol	*Meaning*
AMBULANCE	attention to health, or a health emergency for you or a loved one
My Definition	_____
AMUSEMENT PARK	playtime; pleasurable diversion
My Definition	_____
ANCHOR	staying still; holding steady, secure
My Definition	_____
ANGEL	angelic protection or guidance
My Definition	_____
ANT	teamwork; "busy, busy"; able to carry more than own weight
My Definition	_____
ANTENNA	receiving or sending information or messages
My Definition	_____
APPLAUSE	a job well done; approval; achieved goal
My Definition	_____
APPLE	forbidden fruit, temptation; or preventative medicine ("an apple a day")
My Definition	_____

Symbol	Meaning
APPLE, falling from the tree	traits similar to those of parents
My Definition	_____
APRON STRINGS	immature; "momma's boy" or girl
My Definition	_____
ARM	extension, reaching for more; body part
My Definition	_____
ARMADILLO	armor is on; defensiveness
My Definition	_____
ARROW	taking aim; shooting for a goal; pointing to a direction
My Definition	_____
ATHLETE	above average in sports or exercise
My Definition	_____
ATTIC	in your head; items in attic show how you are thinking
My Definition	_____
ATTIC, cluttered	need to clear out thinking
My Definition	_____

Symbol	*Meaning*
AUDIENCE	on display, or working in front of an audience
My Definition	_____
AUTUMN	time of year
My Definition	_____
AVALANCHE	frozen emotions breaking free or about to come crashing down
My Definition	_____
AWARD	a job well done; approval; achieved goal
My Definition	_____

B

Symbol	*Meaning*
BABY	new beginning; new opportunity; pregnancy
My Definition	_____
BABY'S BREATH, the flower	innocence; gentleness
My Definition	_____
BACK	back problems; the past
My Definition	_____
BACKPACK, walking with one	hiking; enjoying outdoors
My Definition	_____

Symbol	Meaning
BACKPACK, overloaded	carrying a heavy load; great responsibility
My Definition	_____
BACKWARD WORDS	possible learning disability
My Definition	_____
BACKYARD	the past
My Definition	_____
BAGGAGE at back door	unresolved issues from the past
My Definition	_____
BAIT	a lure; enticement
My Definition	_____
BAIT, cutting from line	letting go; time to get out
My Definition	_____
BALCONY	rising above it; higher viewpoint
My Definition	_____
BALD	physical description
My Definition	_____
BALL, bouncing	bouncing around on a decision; indecisive
My Definition	_____

Symbol	Meaning
BALL, dribbling	in control and unwilling to let go
My Definition	_____
BALLOON	floating free; going to burst your bubble; full of hot air
My Definition	_____
BANANA being peeled	peeling back the layers
My Definition	_____
BANANA PEEL on ground	watch your step; beware of slipping
My Definition	_____
BANDAGES	nursing wounds
My Definition	_____
BAND-AID	trying to put a mere Band-Aid on a bad situation
My Definition	_____
BANK	"you can take it to the bank"; money coming or going
My Definition	_____
BANQUET	buffet of choices; indulge, feast
My Definition	_____

Symbol	*Meaning*
BAPTISM	initiation into spiritual consciousness; baptism event
My Definition	_____
BARRICADE	not the way to go; redirect elsewhere
My Definition	_____
BASEBALL	active in this sport
My Definition	_____
BASEMENT	subconscious
My Definition	_____
BASKET, empty	waiting to receive
My Definition	_____
BASKET, full	pay attention to the load you carry
My Definition	_____
BASKETBALL	active in this sport
My Definition	_____
BASKETBALL, shooting	going for the goal; taking the chance
My Definition	_____
BASKETBALL, dribbling	unwilling to let go or to turn something over to someone else
My Definition	_____

Symbol	Meaning
BATH or shower	will be or in need of cleansing; clearing
My Definition	_____
BATTERY, plus or minus sign	charged and ready to go, or needing to recharge
My Definition	_____
BATTLE	up in arms; argument
My Definition	_____
BEACH	time to relax
My Definition	_____
BEAR	grouchy; or in reference to a large man\ (a "bear of a man")
My Definition	_____
BEAR, teddy	cuddly, feeling of security
My Definition	_____
BEARD	hiding something of themselves
My Definition	_____
BEAUTY SHOP	needing a self-esteem boost or makeover (mental or physical)
My Definition	_____

Symbol	Meaning
BEAVER	building emotional dams; blocking things to protect oneself
My Definition	_____
BED or BEDROOM	time to rest; attention to self-care
My Definition	_____
BEE	something is going to sting; gossip-spreader (as a bee flits flower to flower)
My Definition	_____
BELL	"the bell tolls for you"; an alert
My Definition	_____
BELT, pulling tight	tighten finances
My Definition	_____
BIBLE	an interest in religion; religious or spiritual learning
My Definition	_____
BICYCLE	balance; recreation
My Definition	_____
BILL	a debt owed
My Definition	_____
BILLBOARD	a big message in your face
My Definition	_____

Symbol	*Meaning*
BINOCULARS	take a closer look; examination needed
My Definition	_____
BIRD	receiving or delivering messages
My Definition	_____
BIRD on fence	not time yet
My Definition	_____
BIRD, letting go of	setting someone or something free
My Definition	_____
BIRD sitting in hand	keep the sure thing ("a bird in in the hand is worth two in the bush")
My Definition	_____
BIRTH	new opportunity; new beginning
My Definition	_____
BIRTHDAY or WEDDING CAKE	celebration in some area of your life
My Definition	_____
BITE into something	get deeper into project, event, or moment
My Definition	_____
BLACKSMITH standing over coals	forging new strength
My Definition	_____

Symbol	Meaning
BLANKET	covered; secure
My Definition	_____
BLIND	not seeing the point; blind to what's around
My Definition	_____
BLIND, with a cane	slowly feeling the way around
My Definition	_____
BLINDFOLDED	being kept from seeing or knowing
My Definition	_____
BLIZZARD	emotional chaos; not able to see clearly
My Definition	_____
BLOOD	energy given or taken
My Definition	_____
BOARDS for construction	about to build something new
My Definition	_____
BOAT	the emotional self; skimming over emotions
My Definition	_____

Symbol	Meaning
BODY PART	a health problem with the body part you see
My Definition	_____
BOIL	unhealthy emotions surfacing
My Definition	_____
BOMB with a fuse lit	about to explode; an explosive situation that could blow up in your face
My Definition	_____
BONE, throwing to a dog	give someone an opportunity
My Definition	_____
BOOK	new learning; education; time for study
My Definition	_____
BOTTLE, baby	nurturing
My Definition	_____
BOTTLE in ocean	message coming
My Definition	_____
BOW, in archery	person enjoys archery
My Definition	_____
BOW, a ribbon	recognition; award
My Definition	_____

Symbol	Meaning
BOW, gesture from the waist	respect given or shown
My Definition	_____
BOX	containment; boxed in
My Definition	_____
BOXES packed	moving
My Definition	_____
BRAID	entwined; woven together
My Definition	_____
BRAIN	a smart person; health-related (if problem shown)
My Definition	_____
BRAKE	put on the brakes, stop; or out of control, no brakes
My Definition	_____
BRANCH of a tree	an extension of self or of something
My Definition	_____
BRANCH that breaks in the middle	severance or break between something or someone
My Definition	_____

Symbol	*Meaning*
BREAD	nourishment; fellowship, breaking bread
My Definition	_____
BREASTFEEDING	ultimate nourishment
My Definition	_____
BREATH, taking a deep	pause; stop and think about it
My Definition	_____
BREEZE	breath of fresh air
My Definition	_____
BRICK	building a wall between; solid foundation or path
My Definition	_____
BRIDGE	connects one to another; transition to new life or situation
My Definition	_____
BROKEN HEART	disappointment; romantic rejection
My Definition	_____
BROOK	soothing
My Definition	_____
BROOM	sweep it out; clear it out
My Definition	_____

Symbol	*Meaning*
BRUSH	untangle
My Definition	_____
BUBBLE	protecting or shielding yourself; or going to burst your bubble
My Definition	_____
BUD of a flower	about to bloom
My Definition	_____
BUDDHA	meditation; religious belief
My Definition	_____
BUFFET	abundant nourishment; take your pick
My Definition	_____
BUG	small irritation
My Definition	_____
BULL	stubborn, bullheaded; will charge at you
My Definition	_____
BULL in a china shop	not watching what you are doing; crashing about
My Definition	_____
BULLDOZER	moving through obstacles; being run over
My Definition	_____

Symbol	*Meaning*
BURGLAR	stealing items or energy
My Definition	_____
BURIAL	something needs to be put to rest
My Definition	_____
BUS	group transportation; group work
My Definition	_____
BUTCHER	something is being done poorly
My Definition	_____
BUTTER	buttering someone up
My Definition	_____
BUTTERFLY	transformation; freed from restriction
My Definition	_____
BUZZARD	scavenger; picking the bones clean; feeding off others
My Definition	_____

C

CABIN in the woods	need to get away from it all; vacation destination
My Definition	_____

Symbol	*Meaning*
CABLE	conduit for receiving and passing messages or energy
My Definition	
CACTUS	prickly person who will prick you; endurance in any condition
My Definition	
CAGE	being penned in; limitations; self-created confinement
My Definition	
CAKE	special occasion; having your cake and eating it too
My Definition	
CALENDAR	look for month and or day on calendar shown
My Definition	
CAMEL	stamina; you will get there; draw upon inner strength
My Definition	
CAMERA	view life through a different lens; photographer
My Definition	
CAMOUFLAGE	hiding self from others; hunter
My Definition	

Symbol	Meaning
CANDLE	providing light or guidance; spiritual illumination
My Definition	_____
CANDLE with both ends lit	burning the candle at both ends; overextending yourself
My Definition	_____
CANDY	indulgent pleasure; person eats too much sugar
My Definition	_____
CANE	additional support given or needed
My Definition	_____
CAP (hat)	hiding thoughts
My Definition	_____
CAPSIZE	overturned emotionally
My Definition	_____
CAR	physical self (pay attention to the condition of the car and who's driving)
My Definition	_____
CARDS	a game; a gamble
My Definition	_____

Symbol	Meaning
CARPENTER	profession; building or repairing something in life
My Definition	_____
CARROT dangling	motivation
My Definition	_____
CASKET	ending; closed and done
My Definition	_____
CASTLE	fortified against attacks; secure
My Definition	_____
CAT	female part of self; agile
My Definition	_____
CAT on a hot tin roof	in a difficult or hot situation
My Definition	_____
CATERPILLAR	prior to cocoon and rebirth; not yet coming into own
My Definition	_____
CAUTION SIGN	need to be cautious; slow down
My Definition	_____

Symbol	_Meaning_
CAVE	parts of you unexplored; not yet ready to be revealed
My Definition	_____
CEILING	hit your limit; stopping point
My Definition	_____
CEMETERY or GRAVEYARD	final end; not going to rise again
My Definition	_____
CHAIN	many working together; linking together
My Definition	_____
CHAIR	support given; take a load off
My Definition	_____
CHAMELEON	able to adapt; blend in
My Definition	_____
CHAMPAGNE	celebration
My Definition	_____
CHART	objectives or goals
My Definition	_____
CHECK	paying what's owed; rewarded
My Definition	_____

Symbol	Meaning
CHECKERS	game playing; staying one jump ahead
My Definition	_____
CHEERLEADER	cheering you on; "you can do it!"
My Definition	_____
CHEF	profession; likes to cook
My Definition	_____
CHESS	mental or strategic game playing
My Definition	_____
CHEST of the body	body part
My Definition	_____
CHEST (box)	stored or hidden treasure
My Definition	_____
CHEWING	thinking, mulling it over
My Definition	_____
CHICKEN	fearful; lacking self-esteem
My Definition	_____
CHILD	inner child; have children; childish
My Definition	_____

Symbol	*Meaning*
CHOCOLATE	guilty pleasure; decadence
My Definition	_____
CHOIR	group in harmony
My Definition	_____
CHOKING	having trouble accepting; choking on doing something
My Definition	_____
CHRISTMAS	time of year, time for giving
My Definition	_____
CHURCH	a need for reverence
My Definition	_____
CIGAR or CIGARETTE	someone who smokes
My Definition	_____
CIRCLE	coming full circle; circle of life; continuous
My Definition	_____
CIRCLE, standing on the outside of	outside looking in; cut off from others
My Definition	_____
CIRCUS	chaos; too much going on in your life
My Definition	_____

Symbol	Meaning
CLAM	closed off; no communication; keeping it locked inside
My Definition	_____
CLAMP	held together
My Definition	_____
CLASSROOM	group instruction; learning space; education
My Definition	_____
CLAY	can be or is being reshaped
My Definition	_____
CLEARING OFF DESK	clearing out; getting ready for something new
My Definition	_____
CLIFF	pushed to limit; take a leap of faith
My Definition	_____
CLIMB	upward (or downward) movement through effort
My Definition	_____
CLOCK	interpret time showing (using your numbers)
My Definition	_____

Symbol	*Meaning*
CLOSET	hidden or stored away personality traits
My Definition	_____
CLOTHES	the different personality roles worn in public
My Definition	_____
CLOTHESLINE	hung out to dry; air out
My Definition	_____
CLOUD, fluffy white	floating above it all
My Definition	_____
CLOUD, dark overhead	depression
My Definition	_____
CLOUD with a silver lining	a plus to the negative
My Definition	_____
CLOUD, thunderclouds	emotional downpour on horizon
My Definition	_____
CLOWN	personality description; sadness behind the mask
My Definition	_____
COAT	protection
My Definition	_____

Symbol	Meaning
COBWEBS	caught up in old patterns
My Definition	_____
COCK CROWING	time to wake up
My Definition	_____
COCKROACH	personality description
My Definition	_____
COCOON	on cusp of transformation; waiting period before completion
My Definition	_____
COFFEE	stimulating; caffeine habit
My Definition	_____
COFFIN	an ending; put it to rest
My Definition	_____
COINS	money; abundance
My Definition	_____
COLLEGE	advanced learning
My Definition	_____
COLORS	_see chapter 4 and separate list of color meanings at end of dictionary_
My Definition	_____

Symbol	*Meaning*
COMB	untangle; work through it
My Definition	_____
COMPASS	direction needed; direction shown
My Definition	_____
COMPUTER	computer problem; programed way of thinking
My Definition	_____
CONDOM	protection against; barrier between
My Definition	_____
CONDUCTOR on a train	directing others
My Definition	_____
CONDUCTOR, electrical	allows energy to flow through it
My Definition	_____
CONSTRUCTION	building or repairing something in your life; profession
My Definition	_____
CONVENT	cloistering self; restraining or restricting
My Definition	_____

Symbol	Meaning
CONVENTION	like minds joining together; attending convention
My Definition	_____
COOK	preparing something that will feed you; profession
My Definition	_____
COOKBOOK	follow instructions
My Definition	_____
CORK	plug it; "put a cork in it"
My Definition	_____
COUCH, psychiatrist's	look inside for answers
My Definition	_____
COURT	judge, judging others; defendant, being judged
My Definition	_____
COW being milked	nourishment given
My Definition	_____
COYOTE	trickster; pranks
My Definition	_____

Symbol	_Meaning_
CRAB	bad mood ("crabby"); lateral movement
My Definition	_____
CRACK	about to break through
My Definition	_____
CRADLE	place of origin; beginning
My Definition	_____
CRAYONS	color inside the lines; artistic
My Definition	_____
CREAM (dairy)	the best; the top; richness
My Definition	_____
CREDIT CARD	receive it now but pay for it later with interest
My Definition	_____
CRICKET	makes a lot of irritating noise
My Definition	_____
CROSS	burden, a cross to bear; religious; a debt owed
My Definition	_____
CROSSROAD	at a crossroad in life; new direction
My Definition	_____

Symbol	Meaning
CROW	transformation; mediator between life and death
My Definition	_____
CROWN	achievement; king complex
My Definition	_____
CRUISE, boat	have been or are going on a cruise
My Definition	_____
CRUTCH	relying on support rather than standing on one's own
My Definition	_____
CUPID	love at first sight
My Definition	_____
CURTAINS, closed	closing out the world
My Definition	_____
CURTAINS opening	mystery revealed
My Definition	_____
CUT	it's going to cut
My Definition	_____

Symbol	*Meaning*

D

DAISY

simple yet enduring

   My Definition _____

DAM

blocked-up emotions

   My Definition _____

DANCE

joyful expression

   My Definition _____

DARK

unknown; hidden

   My Definition _____

DART

aim for center

   My Definition _____

DAWN

new beginning

   My Definition _____

DEAF, hands over ears

doesn't want to hear truth; avoidance

   My Definition _____

DECK on a house

relax outdoors

   My Definition _____

Symbol	Meaning
DEER	gentleness
My Definition	
DENTIST	need to visit dentist; possible profession
My Definition	
DEPOSIT SLIP	investing money, emotion, or time; need to save money
My Definition	
DESERT	no end in sight; barren; no growth
My Definition	
DETECTIVE	looking for answers
My Definition	
DESK	work; study
My Definition	
DEVIL	temptation
My Definition	
DIAMOND	brilliant; many facets; "diamond in the rough"
My Definition	
DIARY	private thoughts; need to journal
My Definition	

Symbol	Meaning
DICE	it's a gamble
My Definition	_____
DICTIONARY	need definition or clarity
My Definition	_____
DINING or BREAKFAST TABLE	fellowship of family and friends for nourishment
My Definition	_____
DINOSAUR	archaic; prehistoric
My Definition	_____
DIPLOMA	completed a lesson; education; graduation
My Definition	_____
DIRT	grounding; foundation
My Definition	_____
DITCH	stuck in a rut; off your path
My Definition	_____
DOCTOR	health issue; profession; healing needed or given
My Definition	_____

Symbol	Meaning
DOCK	rest; offload; load up
My Definition	_____
DOG	loyal; unconditional love; protective
My Definition	_____
DOLL	fake; someone pretending to be other than who they are
My Definition	_____
DOLPHIN	playful; telepathic communication; spontaneity
My Definition	_____
DOOR, opened	invitation; open to you; opportunity
My Definition	_____
DOOR, closed	closed to you; not for you
My Definition	_____
DOOR, knocking on	opportunity knocking
My Definition	_____
DOOR KNOB turning	opportunity about to open
My Definition	_____
DOORMAT	letting someone walk on or use you
My Definition	_____

Symbol	*Meaning*
DONKEY	obstinate; mulish
My Definition	_____
DOVE	love; peace; divine message coming
My Definition	_____
DRAGON	always roaring; aggressive person
My Definition	_____
DRAGONFLY	transformation; change; good luck
My Definition	_____
DRAWER	see what's in drawer
My Definition	_____
DROWNING	emotions overwhelming you
My Definition	_____
DRUGS	addiction
My Definition	_____
DRUM	communication; walks to beat of their own drum
My Definition	_____
DUCK (bird)	let negative words or emotions roll off
My Definition	_____

Symbol	*Meaning*
DUNCE CAP	not thinking clearly; acted out (if sitting in corner)
My Definition	
DUSK	coming to a close or end
My Definition	
DWARF	letting something overshadow you ("dwarf" you)
My Definition	
DYNAMITE	explosive situation; about to explode
My Definition	

E

EAGLE	soaring; majestic spirit
My Definition	
EAR	listen for message; body part
My Definition	
EARTH	encompasses more than you and your area
My Definition	
EARTHQUAKE	will seriously affect foundation
My Definition	

Symbol	Meaning
EARTHWORM	deeply grounded; of the earth
My Definition	_____
EASTER	resurrection; spring; time of year
My Definition	_____
EGG	about to hatch something new
My Definition	_____
ELASTIC BAND	need to be flexible; extended
My Definition	_____
ELBOW	need to bend; body part
My Definition	_____
ELEPHANT	long or good memory
My Definition	_____
ELEVATOR	going up or down in a situation; moving up or down a level
My Definition	_____
ELF	fun-loving; mischievous
My Definition	_____
EMERALD	healing ability; crystal
My Definition	_____

Symbol	Meaning
EMPTY	self-explanatory
My Definition	
ENGAGEMENT RING	committing to person or project
My Definition	
ENVELOPE	message coming; not shown
My Definition	
ESCALATOR	*see* Elevator *above*
My Definition	
EXERCISE	does or needs exercise
My Definition	
EXIT SIGN	time to leave
My Definition	
EXPERIMENT	step out of comfort zone; time for something new
My Definition	
EXPLOSION	outburst due to suppressed emotions
My Definition	
EYE or EYES	open your eyes; body part
My Definition	

Symbol	Meaning
EYE, third eye	spiritual insight
My Definition	
EYES squinting	can't see clearly; take a closer look
My Definition	

F

Symbol	Meaning
FAN	circulate; cool off
My Definition	
FARM	raised on a farm; enjoys country life
My Definition	
FATHER	parent; mature or masculine aspect of self
My Definition	
FAUCET on	emotions flowing
My Definition	
FAUCET off	emotions turned off
My Definition	
FEATHER	divine guidance; special blessing; feather in cap, ticklish
My Definition	

Symbol	Meaning
FENCE	boundary; fenced in
My Definition	
FIDDLE (musical instrument)	lively
My Definition	
FIELD, running through	sense of freedom
My Definition	
FIGHT	conflict; altercation
My Definition	
FILM	replaying past
My Definition	
FINGER	shows direction; body part
My Definition	
FINGER, shaking at	censure
My Definition	
FINGERS being pried open	won't let go
My Definition	
FINISH LINE	winner; project completed
My Definition	

Symbol	*Meaning*
FIRE	energy; going to burn
My Definition	_____
FIRE, stomping out	put out fire before it's out of control
My Definition	_____
FIRECRACKER	quick-tempered personality
My Definition	_____
FIREMAN	assistance coming; profession
My Definition	_____
FIREWORKS	celebratory display
My Definition	_____
FISH	sustenance; something's fishy; Christian religion
My Definition	_____
FISH out of water	ill at ease
My Definition	_____
FISHING ROD	person likes to fish; relaxation; fishing for answers
My Definition	_____
FIST	hard-hitting
My Definition	_____

Symbol	Meaning
FLAG waving	white, surrender; red, danger
My Definition	
FLAMINGO	digging through the muck for food; rehashing old mistakes
My Definition	
FLASHLIGHT	illuminating path; shining light on something
My Definition	
FLOOD	emotionally overcome
My Definition	
FLOOR	foundation
My Definition	
FLOWER opening	opening up; blossoming
My Definition	
FLUTE	hypnotic; relaxing; plays instrument
My Definition	
FLY (insect)	irritant; something bugging you
My Definition	
FLYING	freedom; have moved above it all
My Definition	

Symbol	*Meaning*
FOG	dazed; unable to see clearly
My Definition	_____
FOOT	physical foundation; body part
My Definition	_____
FOOTBALL	active in this sport
My Definition	_____
FOOTPRINTS	looking back at where you've been
My Definition	_____
FOREHEAD wrinkled	concerned; worried; worries too much
My Definition	_____
FOREST	abundant growth; lost; can't see forest for the trees
My Definition	_____
FORK in road	directional choice to make
My Definition	_____
FOUNTAIN	healing; fount of information
My Definition	_____
FOX	cunning; manipulative
My Definition	_____

Symbol	*Meaning*
FRAGILE icon	handle with care
My Definition	_____
FREEZER	emotions are on ice
My Definition	_____
FROG	hopping from one to another; jumping around on a decision
My Definition	_____
FRONT YARD	future
My Definition	_____
FROZEN	emotionally shut off; cold personality
My Definition	_____
FRUIT	best of life; the fruits of life
My Definition	_____
FUNERAL	ending; letting old go
My Definition	_____

G

GARBAGE	time to throw it out; clear out useless or old thoughts
My Definition	_____

Symbol	Meaning
GARDEN without weeds	positive results from hard work
My Definition	_____
GARDEN with weeds	clear out what's no longer needed
My Definition	_____
GAS GAUGE	shows level done or to be done; measures energy level
My Definition	_____
GAS STATION	refuel energy
My Definition	_____
GATE, closed	blocked
My Definition	_____
GATE, open	previous block open
My Definition	_____
GAVEL	call to order, call for attention, decision final
My Definition	_____
GEESE	protects family; loyalty; monogamous
My Definition	_____
GERBIL	stuck on the wheel, running around
My Definition	_____

Symbol	Meaning
GENERATOR	back-up energy given
My Definition	_____
GEYSER	emotional breakthrough
My Definition	_____
GHOST	shadow of themselves; less than before
My Definition	_____
GIFT	blessing from your higher power
My Definition	_____
GIRAFFE	far-seeing vision; far-reaching
My Definition	_____
GIRDLE	constrained; holding it in
My Definition	_____
GLASS half empty	sees situation in negative light
My Definition	_____
GLASS two-thirds full	sees situation in positive light
My Definition	_____
GLASSES	able to see what couldn't be seen before
My Definition	_____

Symbol	*Meaning*
GLOVE	a good fit
My Definition	_____
GLOVE, boxing	ready for a fight
My Definition	_____
GLUE	stuck; stick to it
My Definition	_____
GNAT	tiny irritant
My Definition	_____
GOAT	going to get your goat, irritate you; butting heads
My Definition	_____
GOLD COINS	money; abundance
My Definition	_____
GOOSE with a golden egg	can deliver abundance, success, or health
My Definition	_____
GRADUATION CAP or GOWN	accomplishment; promotion; move to next level
My Definition	_____
GRAPES	cluster; group together
My Definition	_____

Symbol	Meaning
GREASE	slippery; watch your step
My Definition	_____
GREEN LIGHT	yes; go; do it
My Definition	_____
GROCERY STORE	resource options; variety
My Definition	_____
GUARD at gate	not for you; no entry; a medium's gatekeeper
My Definition	_____
GUINEA PIG	test subject; experimentation
My Definition	_____
GUITAR	plays guitar; musical ability
My Definition	_____

H

Symbol	Meaning
HAIR	physical description
My Definition	_____
HALLOWEEN	time of year; remembering those who passed
My Definition	_____

Symbol	Meaning
HALLWAY	path to multiple doors
My Definition	_____
HAM	personality description ("you're such a ham")
My Definition	_____
HAMMER	delivers an impact, hammer it home
My Definition	_____
HAMMOCK	time to relax
My Definition	_____
HAMSTER	stuck on the wheel, running around
My Definition	_____
HAND	body part
My Definition	_____
HAND over mouth	be quiet
My Definition	_____
HAND,(palm up	receive
My Definition	_____
HAND, sitting on	need patience; wait
My Definition	_____

Symbol	Meaning
HANDCUFFS	bound; confined; limited
My Definition	_____
HAT	hiding thoughts
My Definition	_____
HAWK	predator; aggressive; competitive
My Definition	_____
HEAD, in box	close-minded; can't think outside the box
My Definition	_____
HEADLIGHTS	see what's in front of you
My Definition	_____
HEART	love; body part
My Definition	_____
HEART, broken	heartache; hurt feelings; disappointment
My Definition	_____
HEART, concrete	hard-hearted
My Definition	_____
HEART, frozen	cold to something, someone, or some situation
My Definition	_____

Symbol	Meaning
HEDGEHOG	prickly, nocturnal, solitary by nature
My Definition	_____
HEEL	Achilles' heel; vulnerable area
My Definition	_____
HELICOPTER	rise above situation; take a wider view
My Definition	_____
HELMET	protecting thoughts
My Definition	_____
HEN	overbearing; overprotective
My Definition	_____
HERD	following the crowd
My Definition	_____
HILL	extra effort to reach goal
My Definition	_____
HIP	body part
My Definition	_____
HOE	turning over your foundation; prepping to plant new seeds
My Definition	_____

Symbol	Meaning
HOLE in something	repair needed
My Definition	_____
HOLE in ground	watch your step
My Definition	_____
HOME PLATE (baseball)	stepping up to the plate
My Definition	_____
HONEY	nectar from hard work (for busy bees)
My Definition	_____
HOOD	doesn't want to be seen; hiding who they are
My Definition	_____
HOOK	person is hooked; brought into something without approval
My Definition	_____
HORN	blow your own horn; alarm warning; starter notice
My Definition	_____
HORSE	strength; power; enjoys riding horses
My Definition	_____

Symbol	*Meaning*
HOSPITAL	place of healing; healing needed
My Definition	_____
HOTEL	temporary housing
My Definition	_____
HOUSE	reflective of inner state; a messy house, jumbled thoughts; moving furniture in house, shifting how you think
My Definition	_____
HUMMINGBIRD	sipping the nectar or sweetness of life
My Definition	_____
HUNTING	searching for what nourishes you
My Definition	_____
HURDLE	delays and obstacles
My Definition	_____
HURRICANE	emotional upheaval
My Definition	_____
HYPNOTIZED	in a trance; manipulated by someone; in an altered state
My Definition	_____

Symbol	Meaning

I

ICE

frozen emotions

My Definition _____

ICEBERG

seeing only a small part of the emotional picture

My Definition _____

ICICLE dripping

melting emotions; thawing out

My Definition _____

INDIAN

medicine man; higher guidance; person's heritage

My Definition _____

INDIAN with war paint

on the war path; going to battle

My Definition _____

INDICATOR LIGHT, check engine

have your health checked

My Definition _____

INDICATOR LIGHT, right turn

move forward on a choice or decision

My Definition _____

INK

long-lasting; permanent

My Definition _____

Symbol	Meaning
IRON	smooth out wrinkles
My Definition	_____
ISLAND	isolated; need solitude; escape from life
My Definition	_____

J

Symbol	Meaning
JAIL	restricted; limited; confined
My Definition	_____
JAR	contained
My Definition	_____
JESUS	master guide; religious
My Definition	_____
JOG	person jogs; moving along at comfortable pace
My Definition	_____
JOURNAL	record journey; need to journal
My Definition	_____
JUDGE in his robes	judging self or others
My Definition	_____

Symbol	Meaning
JUGGLE	too many things going at one time
My Definition	_____
JUMP	take the leap
My Definition	_____
JUNGLE	disorder; lost; strongest survive
My Definition	_____
JURY	feel as if others are judging you
My Definition	_____

K

Symbol	Meaning
KANGAROO POUCH	something's hidden
My Definition	_____
KARMA	what goes around comes around
My Definition	_____
KEY	unlock or lock; key to what you want
My Definition	_____
KING	feels above others; top person in family, group, or company
My Definition	_____

Symbol	*Meaning*
KISS on cheek	affection
My Definition	_____
KISS on mouth	love
My Definition	_____
K.I.S.S.	"keep it simple, silly"
My Definition	_____
KITCHEN	in preparation stage; cooking something up
My Definition	_____
KITE	flying free
My Definition	_____
KNEE	time to bend; body part
My Definition	_____
KNEELING	humbled; respect given
My Definition	_____
KNIFE	severing something; will cut to quick
My Definition	_____
KNITTING	connecting; networking; mending
My Definition	_____

Symbol	Meaning
KNOCKING	opportunity knocking
My Definition	_____
KNOTS	tied in knot; binding; disentangle situation
My Definition	_____

L

Symbol	Meaning
LABEL	tagging someone or something negatively or positively
My Definition	_____
LABORATORY	not yet known; in testing stage
My Definition	_____
LADDER	taking one step at a time; up, positive; down, negative
My Definition	_____
LADYBUG	good luck; protection
My Definition	_____
LAKE	emotions (the surface of the water tells the state of emotions)
My Definition	_____

Symbol	*Meaning*
LAMB	gentle as a lamb
My Definition	_____
LAMB on altar	being sacrificed
My Definition	_____
LAMP with shade	doesn't like limelight
My Definition	_____
LAMP with no shade	likes limelight; shines bright
My Definition	_____
LANDSLIDE	foundation shifting or cracking; unexpected shifting event
My Definition	_____
LASER	precise focus; to the point
My Definition	_____
LAUNDRY	cleaning up the persona you show others
My Definition	_____
LAWYER	pleading case; using or needing a lawyer; profession
My Definition	_____
LAXATIVE	time to clean out
My Definition	_____

Symbol	*Meaning*
LEAF, single	need to detach
My Definition	_____
LEAVES on a tree	growth (many leaves are good growth, few leaves are stagnant growth)
My Definition	_____
LEECH	energy being drained
My Definition	_____
LEFT	past; negative; wrong direction
My Definition	_____
LEG	what you stand for; body part
My Definition	_____
LEMON	not good ("that car is a lemon"); situation is sour
My Definition	_____
LENS of a camera	focus
My Definition	_____
LEOPARD	stealth; cunning; can't change their spots
My Definition	_____
LETTER	communication; message
My Definition	_____

Symbol	Meaning
LETTERS, alphabetically reversed	dyslexia; learning disorder
My Definition	_____
LIBRARY	vast knowledge; research needed; search for answers
My Definition	_____
LICENSE	sanctioned; permission to act or move forward
My Definition	_____
LIFE RAFT	temporarily secure; waiting on rescue
My Definition	_____
LIGHT BULB, lit	bright Idea; shines bright
My Definition	_____
LIGHTHOUSE	illuminating your path; will safely guide you
My Definition	_____
LIGHTNING	sudden clarity; sudden illumination
My Definition	_____
LIMB	extension; branching off in new direction
My Definition	_____

Symbol	Meaning
LINK	connects one to another
My Definition	
LION	power; courage; pride
My Definition	
LIVING ROOM	relaxation; social area of home
My Definition	
LIZARD	ability to change and regenerate
My Definition	
LLAMA	carries a load for others
My Definition	
LOCK	protects valuables or secrets
My Definition	
LOCK on door	locked out
My Definition	
LOTUS FLOWER	rebirth; spiritual awakening
My Definition	
LUGGAGE, packing	taking a trip
My Definition	

Symbol	*Meaning*
LUMBER	building or creating something
My Definition	_____

M

Symbol	Meaning
MAGICIAN	duplicitous; misleading; sleight of hand
My Definition	_____
MAGNET	pull things together; strong attraction
My Definition	_____
MAILBOX	message coming
My Definition	_____
MAKEUP	conceal; cover up
My Definition	_____
MANURE	good for growth, will fertilize; full of it
My Definition	_____
MAP	path to follow; see if a location is marked on map
My Definition	_____
MARKET	variety to choose from
My Definition	_____

Symbol	*Meaning*
MASK	hiding behind; hidden; not seeing everything
My Definition	_____
MATCHES	light a fire under self or others
My Definition	_____
MAZE	twists and turns; confusion; don't know which way to go
My Definition	_____
MECHANIC working on car	physical self (= car) needs work
My Definition	_____
MEDICINE	will heal; medicine needed
My Definition	_____
MEDITATION	person meditates; needs meditation
My Definition	_____
MEETING	sharing of information or objectives
My Definition	_____
MERRY-GO-ROUND	stuck in same rut; round and round you go
My Definition	_____

Symbol	*Meaning*
MICROPHONE	speak up; wants to be heard
My Definition	_____
MICROSCOPE	take a closer look
My Definition	_____
MILK	nurturing; allergic; lactose intolerant
My Definition	_____
MINUS SIGN	something negative that will take away from you; a no answer
My Definition	_____
MIRROR	take a closer look at oneself; examine own motives
My Definition	_____
MISTLETOE	Christmastime; hoping for a kiss
My Definition	_____
MOAT	closed off from others; keeps others at a distance
My Definition	_____
MONEY (coins or dollars)	abundance coming
My Definition	_____

Symbol	Meaning
MONK	on path to enlightenment
My Definition	_____
MONKEY	playfulness; curious; ingenuity
My Definition	_____
MONSTER	overblown fears
My Definition	_____
MOON	cleansing energy; illumination
My Definition	_____
MOOSE	power; strength
My Definition	_____
MOSQUITO	will draw blood (energy); irritating sting
My Definition	_____
MOTH	drawn to flame; pulled toward something; could burn you out
My Definition	_____
MOTHBALLS	time to put something away
My Definition	_____
MOUNTAIN, climbing up	work to overcome
My Definition	_____

Symbol	Meaning
MOUNTAIN, climbing down	it's downhill from here
My Definition	_____
MOUSE	quiet; need to listen; descriptive of a person
My Definition	_____
MOUTH	communicate; time to speak up
My Definition	_____
MOVIE	an escape; or movie actions or title describes situation
My Definition	_____
MOVING TRUCK	relocation
My Definition	_____
MUD	mired in perceived limitations; bogged down
My Definition	_____
MULE	hardheaded; stubborn; can carry heavy load
My Definition	_____
MUMMY	past comes back to life; wrapped up in past
My Definition	_____

Symbol	Meaning
MUSCLE	strength; flexing your power; body part
My Definition	_____
MUSEUM	on exhibit; antique
My Definition	_____
MUSICAL NOTE	musical ability
My Definition	_____
MUTE BUTTON	be quiet
My Definition	_____

N

Symbol	Meaning
NAIL in wall or wood	hold or secure something
My Definition	_____
NAIL, striking with a hammer	"you've hit the nail on the head"; you are correct
My Definition	_____
NAKED	all out in the open; feeling exposed
My Definition	_____
NAUSEA	expulsion of negativity
My Definition	_____

Symbol	*Meaning*
NECK	sticking your neck out; body part
My Definition	_____
NEEDLE in a haystack	almost impossible to locate
My Definition	_____
NEEDLE and thread	threading or joining together
My Definition	_____
NEST	preparing for something new; family life
My Definition	_____
NET	caught up in; to catch something
My Definition	_____
NEWSPAPER	interpret news showing in newspaper
My Definition	_____
NIGHTTIME	in the dark; can't see clearly
My Definition	_____
NOSE	strong sense of smell; nosy
My Definition	_____
NOSE with ring in it	being led around by nose
My Definition	_____

Symbol	Meaning
NUMBERS	*see separate list at end of dictionary*
My Definition	
NUDITY	exposure; hiding nudity, uncomfortable with self
My Definition	
NUN	spiritual guide; casts off material things
My Definition	
NURSE	health or healing profession; possible checkup needed
My Definition	
NURSERY	nurturing a new opportunity or life
My Definition	
NUTS	a bit crazy
My Definition	

O

OASIS in a desert	refuge; quenching emotional thirst
My Definition	
OCTOPUS	going in many directions at once; multitasking
My Definition	

Symbol	Meaning
OIL	lubricate; reduce friction
My Definition	_____
OLIVE BRANCH	peace offering; harmony
My Definition	_____
ONION	many layers
My Definition	_____
OPERATION	dig deeper; cut to heart of the problem; surgical operation
My Definition	_____
OPOSSUM	pretending to be something they are not
My Definition	_____
ORANGE	thick-skinned; vitamin C needed
My Definition	_____
ORCHARD	abundant; fruitful
My Definition	_____
ORCHESTRA	working together in harmony
My Definition	_____
ORNAMENT	decoration; touch of glamour
My Definition	_____

Symbol	Meaning
OSTRICH, head buried	avoiding or hiding from something
My Definition	_____
OUTSIDE of something	on outside of situation
My Definition	_____
OWL	wisdom; able to see what others can't
My Definition	_____
OYSTER	hidden value inside
My Definition	_____

P

Symbol	Meaning
PACKAGE at door	delivery coming
My Definition	_____
PADDLE for a boat	will propel forward
My Definition	_____
PAGE, blank	need to make future plans
My Definition	_____
PAINT	fresh look; new feel to life
My Definition	_____

Symbol	Meaning
PAINTBRUSH, artist's	artistic
My Definition	_____
PANTHER	on the prowl; aggressor on the hunt
My Definition	_____
PAPER for wrapping	wrap it up; finish it
My Definition	_____
PARACHUTE	safe to take the dive; support given
My Definition	_____
PARADE	displayed to gain attention
My Definition	_____
PARK	need to go outdoors; relax; family time
My Definition	_____
PARROT	repeats patterns; gossip
My Definition	_____
PARTY	celebration
My Definition	_____
PASSENGER	letting others control your direction; going along for ride
My Definition	_____

Symbol	Meaning
PASSPORT	going out of the country; special ticket to enter
My Definition	_____
PATH	life direction to follow
My Definition	_____
PATIO	step outside situation
My Definition	_____
PEACOCK	bit of a showoff; strut your stuff
My Definition	_____
PEARL	natural hidden talents; wisdom
My Definition	_____
PEDESTAL	recognition; putting someone on a pedestal
My Definition	_____
PEN for writing	ability to communicate through written word
My Definition	_____
PENCIL	short-term; rough draft
My Definition	_____

Symbol	*Meaning*
PENGUIN	yin-yang; yes-no; no gray areas
My Definition	_____
PENDULUM	swings this way then that; indecisive
My Definition	_____
PENTHOUSE	goal reached; at the top
My Definition	_____
PEPPER	spice it up
My Definition	_____
PERFUME	elegant indulgence
My Definition	_____
PERSPIRE	nervous
My Definition	_____
PHOENIX	rebirth, regeneration; strength after loss
My Definition	_____
PHOTO ALBUM, looking through	stuck in past; accept past to move forward
My Definition	_____
PIANO	plays piano; musical ability
My Definition	_____

Symbol	Meaning
PIE	your piece of the pie
My Definition	_____
PIED PIPER	leading others; blindly following
My Definition	_____
PIER	temporarily docking of emotions
My Definition	_____
PIG	wallow in a situation; hogging something
My Definition	_____
PIGEON	messenger; message heading your way
My Definition	_____
PILGRIM	back to the basics; a new start
My Definition	_____
PILL	medicine-related; hard to swallow; is "a pill" (of a personality)
My Definition	_____
PILLAR	stand strong
My Definition	_____
PILLOW	comfort given
My Definition	_____

Symbol	Meaning
PILOT of a boat	control of emotions
My Definition	_____
PILOT of a plane	control of higher learning
My Definition	_____
PIN CUSHION	driving the point home; sticking it to you
My Definition	_____
PIPE	conduit
My Definition	_____
PIRATE	scallywag; thief; will take from you
My Definition	_____
PLANET	circling or rotating around someone or something else
My Definition	_____
PLANT, healthy	growth
My Definition	_____
PLANT, wilting	not caring for something as you should
My Definition	_____
PLANT, dead	no life left in situation or relationship; might also be a dead tree or flower
My Definition	_____

Symbol	Meaning
PLASTIC	fake
My Definition	_____
PLATFORM	means it is about you—pay attention
My Definition	_____
PLOW	reworking foundation
My Definition	_____
PLUMBER	emotional repair needed; profession
My Definition	_____
POCKET	storing away; concealing something
My Definition	_____
POLAR BEAR	perseverance; patience; endurance
My Definition	_____
POLICE	maintain order; assistance given
My Definition	_____
POND, walking beside	disconnected from your emotions
My Definition	_____
PORCH, sitting on	looking to the future
My Definition	_____

Symbol	Meaning
PORCUPINE	prickly; self-protective
My Definition	
POSTER	promote something or someone
My Definition	
POSTMAN or MAIL CARRIER	message being delivered
My Definition	
POUCH, empty	tighten resources
My Definition	
POWDER, baby	reduce friction
My Definition	
POWDER, face	a cover up; covering something up
My Definition	
PRAYING HANDS	requesting guidance; giving gratitude
My Definition	
PREGNANT WOMAN	new life about to emerge
My Definition	
PRESIDENT	leadership
My Definition	

Symbol	Meaning
PRIEST	spiritual teacher
My Definition	_____
PRINCE	younger male
My Definition	_____
PRINCESS	younger female
My Definition	_____
PRISON	confinement; self-confined
My Definition	_____
PRIZE	job well done
My Definition	_____
PUPPET	others in control; being manipulated
My Definition	_____
PUPPY	playful; unconditional love; easily excitable
My Definition	_____
PURSE	contains identity
My Definition	_____
PURSE, empty	watch spending
My Definition	_____

Symbol	Meaning
PUSHED	need to be pushed to do things
My Definition	_____
PUSHING someone	pushing others to do something
My Definition	_____
PUZZLE	working to make pieces fit
My Definition	_____
PYRAMID	spiritual energy given
My Definition	_____

Q

Symbol	Meaning
QUEEN	feminine authority; believes is better than others
My Definition	_____
QUEST	searching for something
My Definition	_____
QUICKSAND	watch your step; surface not as it appears
My Definition	_____
QUILT	protection and warmth given
My Definition	_____

Symbol	Meaning

R

RABBIT

hopping from place to place; jumping around on decision

My Definition _____

RABBIT in a hat

time to pull a rabbit out of the hat

My Definition _____

RACCOON

masked; thief

My Definition _____

RADAR

in your or their sights

My Definition _____

RADIO

communication; receiving information

My Definition _____

RAGS

worn out; no value

My Definition _____

RAILROAD TRACKS

on the right track

My Definition _____

RAIN

emotionally cleansing

My Definition _____

Symbol	Meaning
RAINBOW	blessing given after emotional (cleansing) experience
My Definition	
RAM	ram right into you; headstrong
My Definition	
RAT	sneaky; distrustful
My Definition	
RAVEN	messenger of higher power; harbinger
My Definition	
RAZOR	on the edge; will cut you
My Definition	
RECORD, an LP or 45	you've done it before; repetitious
My Definition	
RED BIRD or ROBIN	harbinger of loved ones and blessings
My Definition	
RED LIGHT	no; stop; don't do it
My Definition	
REEF	barrier
My Definition	

Symbol	Meaning
REFRIGERATOR	chill out; keep your cool
My Definition	_____
RIGHT	forward; future
My Definition	_____
RIPPLE in water	something will have a ripple effect
My Definition	_____
RING, wedding	commitment; bound
My Definition	_____
RIVER	go with the flow
My Definition	_____
ROAD	path you are on (is it bumpy or smooth?)
My Definition	_____
ROBOT	intellect over emotion; habit, routine
My Definition	_____
ROCK	dependable; stable; solid
My Definition	_____
ROCKET	soaring; taking off
My Definition	_____

Symbol	*Meaning*
ROLLER COASTER	lots of ups and downs; get a grip and level out
My Definition	_____
ROOF	protects your thinking
My Definition	_____
ROOSTER	boastful; early riser; head of the henhouse
My Definition	_____
ROOT	get to the bottom of something
My Definition	_____
ROPE around person	confined; at the end of their rope
My Definition	_____
ROPE dangling down	help is coming
My Definition	_____
ROPED OFF	no entry
My Definition	_____
ROSARY	meditative prayer needed
My Definition	_____
ROSE	love in all forms; beauty
My Definition	_____

Symbol	*Meaning*
RUBBER	insulating; flexible
My Definition	_____
RUFFLED FEATHERS	something is or will be irritating
My Definition	_____
RUG	insulating
My Definition	_____
RULER	being measured
My Definition	_____
RUNNING	hobby; runs track; running from something
My Definition	_____
RURAL	simplicity; get back to simple things
My Definition	_____
RUST	past marked or stained
My Definition	_____

S

SAD FACE	disappointment
My Definition	_____

Symbol	Meaning
SADDLE	saddling oneself with unneeded stress or worry; or comfortable fit
My Definition	
SAILBOAT	go with the flow
My Definition	
SAND	change, shifts; shifting, not solid foundation
My Definition	
SANTA CLAUS	time of year; gift coming your way
My Definition	
SATELLITE	communication from higher power
My Definition	
SAW	going back and forth on something
My Definition	
SCALES	balance; weighted one way or the other; scales of justice
My Definition	
SCAR	hurt feelings not healed yet
My Definition	

Symbol	Meaning
SCARECROW	guarding something (in crop field); feels less than others (scarecrow in *The Wizard of Oz*)
My Definition	_____
SCHOOL	lesson to be learned
My Definition	_____
SCIENTIST	investigate; research
My Definition	_____
SCISSORS	cutting away nonessentials; cut to heart of situation
My Definition	_____
SCORPION	poisonous; painful sting
My Definition	_____
SCRIPT for a play	following the script; doing what you are told to do; actor
My Definition	_____
SEAL (animal)	crowd-pleaser
My Definition	_____
SEAL with a ball on its nose	need to balance
My Definition	_____

Symbol	Meaning
SEAL (embossed wax)	approved
My Definition	
SEAM	need to blend and come together
My Definition	
SEAM opening up	coming apart at the seams
My Definition	
SEED	starting a new beginning
My Definition	
SEEDS, planting in soil	new growth
My Definition	
SEESAW	highs and lows; going up and down on something
My Definition	
SHADE	got it made in the shade; relax in the shade
My Definition	
SHADOW	past; hiding in the shadows
My Definition	
SHAMPOO	cleaning or clearing how you think
My Definition	

Symbol	Meaning
SHAVING FACE	removing mask
My Definition	_____
SHARK	will take a painful bite out of you emotionally
My Definition	_____
SHEEP	follows the herd; break out on your own
My Definition	_____
SHELL	closed off in own shell; protection layer around you
My Definition	_____
SHH!	be quiet
My Definition	_____
SICK	releasing negative energy
My Definition	_____
SHIELD	defense; protection
My Definition	_____
SHOE	grounding; foundation
My Definition	_____
SHOES, shining	buffing up your foundation
My Definition	_____

Symbol	*Meaning*
SHOULDER	a chip on the shoulder; defensive
My Definition	_____
SHOVEL	dig in: there's work to be done; digging deep
My Definition	_____
SHOVEL in graveyard	digging your own grave
My Definition	_____
SHOWER	cleansing; clearing
My Definition	_____
SILK	smooth as silk
My Definition	_____
SINGING	harmony; joyful
My Definition	_____
SKATE	skating past responsibilities; activity enjoyed
My Definition	_____
SKELETON	part of your past (skeleton in closet); not as once was
My Definition	_____

Symbol	Meaning
SKIN, blotchy	probable skin condition
My Definition	_____
SKUNK	will leave a stink on you
My Definition	_____
SKY, clear	smooth sailing; the sky's the limit
My Definition	_____
SKY, cloudy	confusion
My Definition	_____
SLATE being wiped	a clean slate
My Definition	_____
SLIDING downhill	going in the wrong direction
My Definition	_____
SLOTH	slow-moving, languid
My Definition	_____
SMOKE or SMOG	can't see way through; move forward with caution
My Definition	_____
SNAIL	slow movement; not moving fast enough
My Definition	_____

Symbol	Meaning
SNAKE	dishonest; will betray or deceive you
My Definition	
SNAPSHOTS	quick impressions; quick decisions
My Definition	
SNEEZE	rejection; getting irritant out of your system
My Definition	
SNOW	not time for planting new; pause in effort
My Definition	
SOAP	time to cleanse mind or body
My Definition	
SOCCER BALL	active in this sport
My Definition	
SOLDIER(S)	military; going to war
My Definition	
SPIDER spinning web	beware of web spun by you or another
My Definition	
SPIDERWEB, completed	caught in or catching in web; watch patterns you create
My Definition	

Symbol	Meaning
SPINE	strong spine or spineless, depending on image; body part
My Definition	_____
SPINNING WHEEL	pick up the threads (of something)
My Definition	_____
SPLINTER	small irritant; don't let it fester
My Definition	_____
SPONGE	absorbs easily; soaks up new learning
My Definition	_____
SPOON	spoon-fed; things are easier
My Definition	_____
SPREADSHEET	analyze; analysis
My Definition	_____
SPRING	season of year; time to plant seeds
My Definition	_____
SQUARE	boxed in; confined
My Definition	_____
SQUIRREL	hoards items; store away
My Definition	_____

Symbol	Meaning
STAG (animal)	ram right into you; headstrong
My Definition	
STAMP (ink)	seal of approval
My Definition	
STAIRS	consciousness direction: up, raising; down, lowering
My Definition	
STAR	star of show; success
My Definition	
STATIONARY BIKE	going nowhere fast
My Definition	
STATUE	beautiful but lifeless
My Definition	
STEEL	strong; inflexible
My Definition	
STEERING WHEEL	take control; in control
My Definition	
STOMACH	having trouble stomaching something; body part
My Definition	

Symbol	Meaning
STOP SIGN	no; stop; don't do it; warning not to proceed
My Definition	_____
STORK	baby coming soon; opportunity being delivered
My Definition	_____
STORM	inner emotional conflict
My Definition	_____
STRANGLE	constricting energy or life flow
My Definition	_____
STRING	stringing something or someone along
My Definition	_____
STUDENT	new learning
My Definition	_____
STUMP	growth severed
My Definition	_____
SUBMARINE	emotions buried; hidden below surface
My Definition	_____
SUGAR cube	sugar addiction
My Definition	_____

Symbol	Meaning
SUITCASE	travel
My Definition	
SUMMER	time of year
My Definition	
SUN	energy; energy given
My Definition	
SUNFLOWER	happiness
My Definition	
SWAMP	bogged down
My Definition	
SWAN	graceful; gliding along
My Definition	
SWIMMING POOL	diving in head first
My Definition	
SWING	going back and forth on something
My Definition	
SWITCH	ability to turn it on or off
My Definition	

Symbol	Meaning
SWORD	defend yourself; double-edged sword
My Definition	_____
SYRINGE	healing injections given; drug problem
My Definition	_____
SYRUP	laying it on too thick
My Definition	_____

T

Symbol	Meaning
TAIL	bringing up the rear
My Definition	_____
TABLE	laying your cards on the table; table it
My Definition	_____
TABLECLOTH, smoothing over	smooth things out; get the wrinkles out
My Definition	_____
TAILOR	creating a new you
My Definition	_____
TANGLE	a mess; tangled-up situation; confusion
My Definition	_____

Symbol	Meaning
TANK	bringing out the big guns
My Definition	_____
TAPE	secure it; patch it
My Definition	_____
TAPESTRY	patterns of life
My Definition	_____
TAPPING FOOT	waiting on something to happen; impatient
My Definition	_____
TARGET	focus on goal
My Definition	_____
TATTOO	permanently mark you; person has tattoo
My Definition	_____
TEA, iced	refreshing
My Definition	_____
TEA, hot	relaxing
My Definition	_____
TEARS	emotional release; cleansing
My Definition	_____

	Symbol	_Meaning_

TEDDY BEAR

cuddly; a softy

My Definition   _____

TEETH

sink your teeth in; grinding; body part

My Definition   _____

TELEGRAM

urgent message

My Definition   _____

TELEPHONE

communication; reaching out

My Definition   _____

TELEPHONE POLES

linked group communication

My Definition   _____

TELEVISION

escape to another world

My Definition   _____

TEMPLE

spiritual connection; sacred

My Definition   _____

TENT

temporary housing; camping

My Definition   _____

THEATER

putting on an act; profession

My Definition   _____

Symbol	*Meaning*
THERMOMETER	gauge emotions; gauge degree reached
My Definition	
THORN	irritating person
My Definition	
THREAD	pull things together; partial truth
My Definition	
THROAT	body part
My Definition	
TIDAL WAVE	overwhelmed; drowning
My Definition	
TIGER	on the prowl; aggressor; tiger by the tail
My Definition	
TIGHTROPE	walking a tightrope; tread carefully; stay balanced
My Definition	
TOILET	need to release; let it go; eliminate
My Definition	
TONGUE, holding	don't speak out
My Definition	

Symbol	Meaning
TOOLS	install new; repairs needed
My Definition	_____
TORCH	handing off to next in line; obsessed with something
My Definition	_____
TORNADO	destructive path
My Definition	_____
TOYS	need to play more
My Definition	_____
TRACKS	on the right path
My Definition	_____
TRAIN	pulling a heavy load
My Definition	_____
TRAIN TRESTLE	support moving over difficult area
My Definition	_____
TRANSPARENT plastic	nothing hidden; see through someone
My Definition	_____
TRAP	beware traps laid; confined
My Definition	_____

Symbol	Meaning
TRAPEZE	flying high
My Definition	_____
TRASH	time to take out the trash
My Definition	_____
TREADMILL	going nowhere fast; stuck in same place
My Definition	_____
TREASURE	abundance
My Definition	_____
TREE	growth; development
My Definition	_____
TRESPASSING	overstepping your bounds
My Definition	_____
TRIANGLE	trinity; power of 3; stages of life
My Definition	_____
TROLLING THE WATER	systematically searching
My Definition	_____
TROPHY	you win; you earned it; appreciation shown
My Definition	_____

Symbol	*Meaning*
TRUCK	hauls heavy load
My Definition	_____
TUG OF WAR	no compromise; back and forth argument
My Definition	_____
TURKEY (bird)	Thanksgiving, time of year
My Definition	_____
TURTLE	slow-moving yet steady; quickly retreats to shell
My Definition	_____

U

UFO	unfamiliar; unknown
My Definition	_____
UMBRELLA	protection from others' emotions; shield
My Definition	_____
UNICORN	innocence; purity
My Definition	_____
UNIFORM	profession-specific clothing
My Definition	_____

Symbol	Meaning
UNIFORM, white hat	navy
My Definition	_____
UNIFORM, green helmet	army
My Definition	_____
UNIFORM, gold wings pin	air force
My Definition	_____
UNIVERSITY or college	higher learning
My Definition	_____

V

VACUUM	suck it up
My Definition	_____
VALLEY	peaceful contemplation; rest and recharge
My Definition	_____
VAMPIRE	person or situation draining energy
My Definition	_____
VAULT	secure it; locked up inside; secrets kept
My Definition	_____

Symbol	Meaning
VEHICLE stuck	stuck in a rut
My Definition	_____
VIOLIN	sensitive; romantic; musically inclined
My Definition	_____
VINE	cling to
My Definition	_____
VISE	squeezed too tight
My Definition	_____
VOLCANO	eruption; volatile personality; negative situation erupts
My Definition	_____
VOMIT	forceful rejection
My Definition	_____
VULTURE	feeds on the weak
My Definition	_____

W

Symbol	Meaning
WAGON, full	carrying a heavy load
My Definition	_____

Symbol	Meaning
WAGON, empty	feel unfulfilled
My Definition	
WALL	blocked
My Definition	
WALLET	contains identity
My Definition	
WALLET, empty	broke; financial problems
My Definition	
WAND	ability to create; wave wand and make it happen
My Definition	
WAR	conflict with others or inside self
My Definition	
WASHBOARD	doing things the hard way; hard work
My Definition	
WASHING HANDS	time to let go; walk away from it
My Definition	
WASP	it's going to sting you
My Definition	

Symbol	*Meaning*
WATCH, checking	concerned with time; repeated number (see Numbers list for meaning)
My Definition	_____
WATER	always emotions
My Definition	_____
WATER, walking beside	detached from your emotions
My Definition	_____
WATERFALL	may become overwhelmed; releasing of emotions
My Definition	_____
WATER, boiling	overly emotional; boiling with anger
My Definition	_____
WAVE	riding highs and lows; going with the flow
My Definition	_____
WAX	easily molded; impressionable
My Definition	_____
WEAPON	protection tool; wrong use of words or manipulation
My Definition	_____

Symbol	*Meaning*
WEASEL	slyness; dishonesty
My Definition	
WEAVE	blending things together
My Definition	
WEB	tangled up in something
My Definition	
WEDDING	joining, blending, or merging together
My Definition	
WEEDS	negatives that need to removed
My Definition	
WELL	deep emotions not revealed
My Definition	
WEST	direction indicator
My Definition	
WHALE	something huge; must go through layers to reach center
My Definition	
WHEAT	nourishment; body unable to process well
My Definition	

Symbol	Meaning
WHEEL	controlling direction; wheel of life
My Definition	_____
WHIP	verbal or physical abuse of self or others
My Definition	_____
WILLOW tree	surrender to emotion (weeping willow)
My Definition	_____
WIND	change (positive or negative) in the wind
My Definition	_____
WINDOW	see through a situation; see into the other side
My Definition	_____
WINGS	taking off; time to soar
My Definition	_____
WHITE-ROBED PERSON	spiritual guide
My Definition	_____
WIRE	connector; connecting
My Definition	_____
WIRED	stressed; anxious
My Definition	_____

Symbol	Meaning
WITCH	cruel manipulative personality
My Definition	
WOLF	need to howl; sneaky; pack mentality
My Definition	
WOOL	soft; warm; comforting
My Definition	
WOOD	building material; fuel for warmth
My Definition	
WORM in the earth	work your way through foundation
My Definition	
WRECK	collision imminent; loss of control; a mess ("she's a wreck")
My Definition	
WRITING	need to journal; profession
My Definition	

X

Symbol	Meaning
X-RAY	ability to see inside; look below the surface
My Definition	

Symbol	Meaning

Y

YAWN

bored; tired

My Definition _____

YARN

spinning a tale; knits

My Definition _____

YEAR

time in life

My Definition _____

YIELD SIGN

slow down; time for compromise

My Definition _____

YIN-YANG

black and white; balance between positive and negative

My Definition _____

YOGA

does or needs yoga

My Definition _____

YOKE

being reined in; harnessed to thought patterns/habits

My Definition _____

YO-YO

highs and lows; up and down

My Definition _____

Symbol	Meaning

Z

ZEBRA

black and white view of life; "it is what it is"

   My Definition _____

ZIP CODE

location

   My Definition _____

ZIPPER

be quiet ("zip it"); close or open things up;

   My Definition _____

ZOMBIE

emotionally vacant

   My Definition _____

ZOO

lacking order

   My Definition _____

BASIC NUMEROLOGY NUMBERS

I didn't provide blank lines in this section to add your own interpretations. This page is the basic numerology interpretation for your knowledge. You are able to add your own number interpretations in the next section.

1	beginnings; individuality; independence; leadership; authority
2	balance; partnership; diplomacy; cooperation
3	creativity; self-expression; communication; social
4	logic; reason; pragmatic; problem solving
5	change; adventure; innovation; freedom; challenge
6	harmony; domestic; community; relationships; service
7	spirituality; growth; metaphysics; solitude; contemplation
8	abundance; manifestation; ambition; goals
9	closure; endings; completion; compassion; wisdom

NUMBERS

The numbers in this section are a combination of numerology, what I was taught, and my own experience. Make these numbers your own.

	Symbol	*Meaning*
0		void; cycle; never ending
	My Definition	_____
1		new beginnings; masculine aspect; leader; independence
	My Definition	_____
2		balance; feminine aspect; diplomacy
	My Definition	_____
3		psychic; creative; trinity; communication
	My Definition	_____
4		foundation; work; practicality; discipline
	My Definition	_____
5		change; versatility; adventure; freedom; innovative
	My Definition	_____

Symbol	Meaning
6	responsibility; family; nurturing; domestic
My Definition	_____
7	intuition; spirituality; lucky 7; meditative; personal growth
My Definition	_____
8	goals; abundance; manifestation; success
My Definition	_____
9	endings; closure; completion
My Definition	_____
13	unlucky; no luck with person or situation
My Definition	_____

Add numbers that are special to you, along with your interpretation of them, in the space below.

COLORS

Symbol	*Meaning*
SILVER	wisdom
My Definition	_____
WHITE	spiritual; purity
My Definition	_____
BLACK	unseen; unknown; power; elegance; formality; mystery
My Definition	_____
BLUE	calm; boy; blue skies; blue mood; moody
My Definition	_____
BROWN	physical; earth; grounding
My Definition	_____
GOLD	valuable
My Definition	_____
GRAY	depression; "blah"; faded out
My Definition	_____

Symbol	*Meaning*
GREEN	healing; growth
My Definition	_____
ORANGE	energy; vibrant
My Definition	_____
PINK	love; girl; gentle
My Definition	_____
PURPLE	regal; royalty; religious; communication
My Definition	_____
RED	passion; dynamic; anger; dramatic; aggressive; warning
My Definition	_____
YELLOW	sunshine; bright; mental; intellectual
My Definition	_____

Add other colors that are special to you, along with your interpretation of them, in the space below.

YOUR SYMBOLS

Use this space to list symbols not in this dictionary that are important to you along with a definition for what they mean to you.

Printed in the United States
by Baker & Taylor Publisher Services